DR JULIE KOKESCH PSY.D.

Hack Aging! Get Younger with Human Design

Disclaimer:

The information in this book is for education and entertainment purposes only and is not intended to be a substitute for professional medical or psychological advice.

First edition

ISBN: 979-8-218-83528-6

This book was professionally typeset on Reedsy.
Find out more at reedsy.com

Contents

VIII References & Resources

Preface

April 2019 was a month etched into my memory—a time of profound transformation. It marked my 50th birthday, a milestone I had anticipated with mixed emotions. But instead of celebration, the month carried the heavy weight of grief. We had just lost Miles, my sisters baby, and the pain was raw. This loss coincided with my Chiron return, a cosmic rite of passage that left me questioning everything about my purpose and is there a god and what the hell is it all about anyway? I felt untethered, as though the universe had conspired to confront me with the realities of aging, mortality, and misalignment all at once.

Amid this emotional whirlwind, I decided to send in my cells for analysis—a decision that would change the trajectory of my anti-aging and biohacking life. When the results came back, I was stunned. My biological age was significantly older than my chronological age. At first, I couldn't believe it. I stared at the report in disbelief and muttered, "Oh f*ck no! This is unacceptable." How could this be possible? I had been sober off and on for years, meticulously detoxing my home from harmful chemicals and fragrances. I ate very clean, exercised regularly, danced with friends, and even worked with hormone specialists to optimize my health. By all accounts, I was doing a sh*t ton right—or so I thought.

That moment was a wake-up call. It wasn't just about losing

Miles or turning 50; it was about realizing that despite all my efforts, something deeper was out of sync. The traditional methods of self-care and biohacking that I had relied on suddenly felt insufficient. All the conditioning and one-size-fits-all bullsh*t was all wrong for my body. Following a vast majority of general suggestions were not working! I stood in front of the mirror, and my blood test results, one morning and saw a reflection that didn't feel like me—older, worn down by grief and time. It was in that moment of vulnerability that I knew I needed to dig deeper but I needed it something that was more unique and specialized to ME. I am different, I am not just one of the herd. I'm a Shepherd not a sheep.

This revelation led me down an unexpected path. I began exploring intermittent fasting, specifically tailored for women in menopause—a practice that not only helped me manage weight but also improved mental clarity and the sense of control. At the same time, I delved into Human Design, a system that helped me before but it was time to take it deeper to help me understand myself on a more profound level. One concept that resonated deeply was "internal markets," and "indirect light" which helped me align my energy with what truly nourishes me or ages me. I started to take these 2 concepts more literal. In a weird way I dumbed it down and started to apply it very practically and thoroughly to every area of my life. Cool vampire story coming up, stay tuned.

The journey wasn't linear; it was filled with trial and error. For your information the trial and error process is also part of my human design chart and I will go in to depth about this process. I took on the attitude of, f*ck it, lets figure out what doesn't work by experimenting and that's how we'll know without a doubt what DOES work. But through this process, three lessons became clear:

1. Loss sucks—it strips you bare and forces you to confront stuff.
2. Knowing yourself can set you free—understanding who you are at your core is trans-formative.
3. Experiment your butt off—success comes from relentless curiosity and willingness to try new things.

Looking back now in September 2025, I see how these pivotal moments reshaped not just my health but also my entire perspective on life. They taught me resilience and the power of personalization in healing—a journey I hope to share with others navigating their own paths to wellness. I/we are our own authorities in the end.

Imagine waking up each day with renewed energy, feeling younger, both in mind and spirit. This book will guide you through discovering how to harness Human Design to not only understand yourself but to enhance your physical and mental well-being. This morning I woke up, jumped on the bicycle to get coffee creamer and I was saying my gratitude list all the way and feeling so high on life, and so f*cking proud of myself that I made the brave choices I made. I love my life today and I don't want to die because I'm finally super excited to be alive and experience more and more.

We will dive into the essentials of Human Design, explore the art of biohacking, and discover how to fuse these concepts into a personalized blueprint for a more youthful, vibrant life. Of course these are all suggestions, ideas and concepts that you will need to do your own experimenting with but if you haven't tried them yet or felt like I did when I got those crappy biological age tests results. Applying your Human Design charts info to your life and biohacking choice, may be the added variable that makes a huge difference for you too.

As you turn these pages, I urge you to adopt a mindset of exploration and curiosity—every individual is unique, including you! Embrace the opportunity to experiment and find what works best in your journey toward renewal and vitality. Finding out what works may sometimes mean your find out what doesn't work but at least you have more data and can move on, more confidently.

Acknowledgments

Thank you to my sisters for your wisdom, creativity, and artistic input — you helped me bring this book across the finish line.

Thank you to my family for your steady love and support through every chapter of my life.

Thank you to my spiritual network of friends — you know who you are — for keeping me grounded, inspired, and connected.

Thank you to the Human Design community of teachers, leaders, and everyday humans who are living authentically and showing what it means to truly decondition.

And thank you to all the doctors and nutritionists who guided me along my biohacking journey — your expertise has been invaluable.

Introduction

Hello and welcome to *Hack Aging and Get Younger with Human Design*.

If you're picking up this book because you're a **biohacker** or curious about biohacking — welcome.

If you're here because you **don't know what Human Design is**, I'll give you a few pointers to get started before we dive in.

And if you're already familiar with **Human Design** but have never considered how we can biohack with it — I invite you to keep an open mind and look at this system through a new lens.

If You're New to Human Design

The first step is to run your chart. You can do this for free at: JovianArchive.com

The International School of Human Design, IHDSchool.com

BG5 Business Institute (the business application of Human Design) BG5businessInstitute.com

Make sure you have your **birth date**, the **city, state, and country** where you were born, and your **exact or best-guess birth time**. Convert to military time if born after noon. (for example 1pm is 13:00) For most of what we'll explore in this book, a good estimate will work. If you don't know your exact time, try contacting the hospital where you were born or writing to the county courthouse to request an original copy of your birth certificate or record of birth (there's usually a small fee).

And if you're thinking, "I was adopted," "I don't have records," or "I was born in a cornfield somewhere"... you're not alone. For cases where birth time is unclear, you can work with a Human Design Analyst or someone who uses **Maia Mechanics Advanced Software,** MaiaMechanics.com, to calculate how strong or weak your birth time reliability is.

By the time this book is out, there may even be trustworthy AI apps — but if you go that route, I highly recommend getting a second opinion from a reliable source. I have emailed many AI app coders making them aware of inaccuracies.

I have the Maia software myself, so feel free to contact me if you'd like me to run your birth time reliability calculation. (Scan the QR code on the last page of this book, to reach me.) Fine-tuning your birth time can make a big difference for the more detailed biohacking applications later in the book.

How to Read This Book

I wrote this book to be **educational and entertaining**. The first half lays out foundational knowledge; the second half is filled with personal stories and lived experimentation. You don't have to read it cover to cover in order — think of it as a toolkit rather than a novel.

Start wherever you're most curious. Use the **Table of Contents**, grab a stack of sticky notes, and jump to the sections that speak to you. Each chapter is designed to stand on its own, so you can absorb the information in whatever sequence feels right.

A Final Welcome

I'm genuinely grateful that you've chosen to be here — whether your motivation is curiosity, longevity, self-discovery, or all three. This book was written for people who want to **know themselves better**, **live longer**, and **live healthier**. I wrote this book to connect with you and support you on your journey. You are not alone.

So take a deep breath, open your chart, and get ready to see yourself — and biohacking — through an entirely new lens.

My Introduction to Human Design

My first encounter with Human Design was... rocky. A friend at ecstatic dance kept bringing it up, but she couldn't explain it well. Honestly, I didn't think she was the sharpest tool in the shed, so I brushed it off. But she was persistent—and eventually, my curiosity won out.

At the time, I had a doctorate in psychology, a dissertation with 75 references, and years of research-based training at UCLA. My brain was trained to demand evidence, citations, peer-reviewed studies. So when she told me Human Design was "who she was," I rolled my eyes. But something in me thought: *Okay, let's investigate.*

I ordered a book by Ra Uru Hu, the founder of Human Design, and ran my chart on Jovian Archive. Suddenly, I was staring at something called a "bodygraph," and apparently, I was a **Projector**. The chart said my strategy was to "wait for the invitation." At the time, I didn't know what that meant—but I recognized the bitter feeling of forcing myself into spaces where I wasn't really wanted. That landed.

The Reading That Set Me on a Journey

Skepticism aside, I booked my first Human Design reading. It cost me $450—steep for something I didn't yet believe in—but it planted a seed I couldn't ignore.

The reader explained: Projectors make up about 21% of the population. We're designed to guide others, not to hustle endlessly. Our success depends on recognition and invitations. Our "not-self" theme? Bitterness.

That word—bitterness—was like a spotlight on my past. The sting of overhearing "too much," the times I felt invisible, the exhaustion of chasing instead of being chosen. Suddenly, it all made sense. For the first time, I felt seen. Validated. Not broken—just different.

That one reading cracked something open. It didn't give me all the answers, but it gave me a new lens to look at myself—and eventually, a whole new way to live.

I

Biohacking & Foundations

1

What is Human Design?

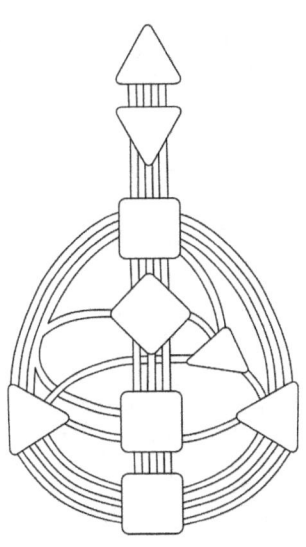

Human Design: A Blueprint for Living in Alignment with Your Authentic Self

Human Design is often referred to as "The Science of Differentiation" because it shows you how uniquely you're wired to live, work, and make decisions. This system blends ancient wisdom with modern science to provide you with a personalized map of your energetic blueprint—a guide to living true to yourself, rather than relying on inherited or cultural expectations.

Ancient Wisdom Meets Modern Science

At its core, Human Design synthesizes elements from multiple ancient traditions, combining them with contemporary scientific discoveries to form a holistic self-knowledge system:

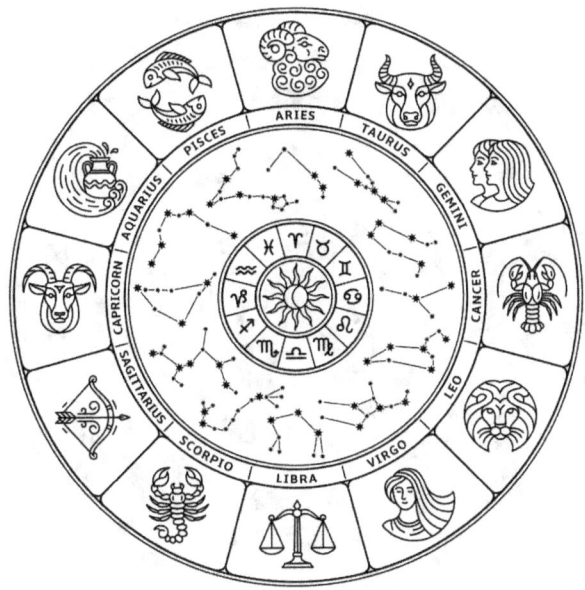

- **Western & Eastern Astrology**: These astrological systems map the planetary influences on your energy, showing how celestial movements shape your personality.

- **Chinese I'Ching**: The 64 hexagrams of the I'Ching are integrated into your chart, corresponding to genetic codons that influence your traits and behaviors.

- **Hindu-Brahmin Chakra System**: Expanded to include nine energy centers, Human Design reflects modern human evolution and the way our bodies process energy.

- **Judaic Kabbalah (Tree of Life)**: This system offers a structural foundation for the BodyGraph, the visual representation of your unique energetic makeup.

In addition to these ancient systems, Human Design incorporates modern disciplines such as **quantum mechanics**, **astronomy**, **genetics**, and **biochemistry** to explain how energy flows through your body and how you can use this knowledge to optimize your life. One of the most fascinating aspects is the role of **neutrinos**—subatomic particles that pass through all matter, carrying information from the universe. These particles imprint on your DNA at the exact moment of your birth, shaping your design.

The BodyGraph: Your Energetic Blueprint

The **BodyGraph** is the visual representation of your Human Design, calculated using your birth data (date, time, and location). It maps out how your energy flows and how you're naturally inclined to interact with the world. It's your unique operating manual.

The BodyGraph consists of:

- **Nine Energy Centers**: These centers represent areas of consistent (defined) or variable (undefined) energy. Some centers are fixed and reliable, while others are more flexible and open to external influence.
- **64 Gates**: Derived from the I'Ching, each gate corresponds to a specific trait or theme, offering insight into your personal strengths, challenges, and life purpose.
- **Channels**: These are the connections between gates, indicating areas of consistent energy flow. Many refer to these as "bridges" that help you understand the continuous flow of energy throughout your body.

Key Concepts: Type, Strategy, and Authority

- **Type**: Your Type (e.g., Manifestor, Generator, Projector, Reflector) describes your natural role in the world and how you're designed to engage with others.
- **Strategy**: Each Type has its own Strategy—guidelines for interacting with the world in a way that feels aligned and natural.
- **Authority**: This is the internal decision-making mecha-

nism that helps you navigate life in a way that feels true to yourself. It's your body's way of signaling which choices are right for you.

Practical Application: Living in Alignment

Human Design isn't about predicting your future—it's about understanding your birth chart and making better decisions in real time. It helps you see where you're forcing strategies that don't work for you and shows you how to live in a way that feels more effortless and natural.

When you're in alignment with your design, life flows with less resistance. You stop trying to fit yourself into boxes that never quite fit and start experiencing greater clarity, success, and peace of mind. Rather than blindly following external rules or societal pressures (conditioning), Human Design empowers you to make choices that honor your true nature.

The Science of Neutrinos

To understand how Human Design works at a quantum level, it's essential to understand neutrinos. These subatomic particles, often called "stardust," stream through everything—including you—at nearly the speed of light. As they pass through you, they leave an energetic imprint on your DNA, shaping your BodyGraph and influencing your personality traits, decisions, and life path. It's a unique blend of ancient wisdom and cutting-edge science that explains why we're all so different and how we can harness those differences for greater harmony and success.

2

How Human Design Works

How Human Design Works: A Practical, Personalized Blueprint

Human Design begins with your **BodyGraph**, a chart created using your birth date, time, and location. At first glance, it might look like a mash-up of a chakra map, a circuit board, and a NASA diagram, but beneath the strange shapes and colors is a personalized blueprint of how your energy operates. It's your owner's manual—specifically for you.

Key Components of Your BodyGraph:

- **Type**: Your core energetic role in the world (e.g., Generator, Manifesting Generator, Manifestor, Projector, Reflector). This tells you how you're naturally designed to interact with the world.
- **Strategy**: Your personalized approach to engaging with the world in a way that reduces resistance. It's your unique way of operating without forcing things.
- **Authority**: Your internal decision-making compass, guiding you in making choices that are aligned with your true

nature. Different Authorities (e.g., Emotional, Sacral) reflect different ways to tune into your body's wisdom.

· **Centers**: Nine energy hubs inspired by the chakra system, showing you where you have consistent energy and where you're influenced by others.

· **Channels & Gates**: The finer details that highlight your strengths, sensitivities, and the recurring themes in your life. These areas reflect what's most consistent and stable about you, as well as what's more malleable and open to external influences.

Human Design isn't a personality quiz, and it doesn't tell you who you "should" be. Instead, it helps you see how you're already functioning—what's working for you and where you've been conditioned to follow paths that aren't truly yours. It's about understanding the energy dynamics at play in your life and learning to navigate them more consciously.

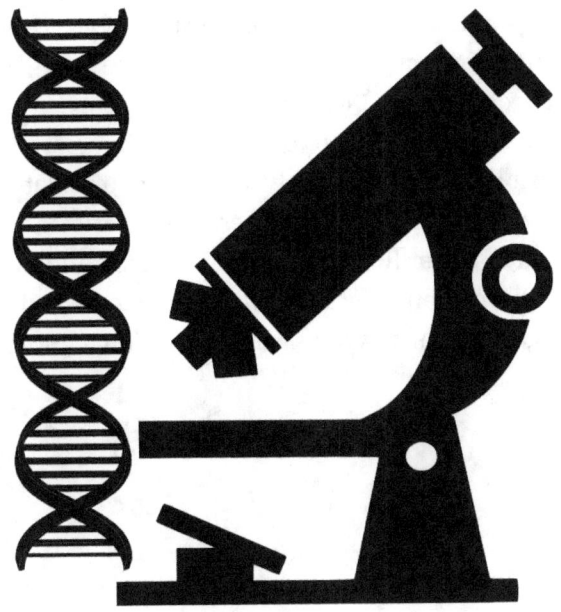

The Experiment: Living Your Design

Here's where it gets powerful: Human Design isn't about mentally "figuring yourself out." The system is practical and rooted in **experimentation**. It's about **testing** how your Type, Strategy, and Authority work in real-life situations. What happens when you start following your Strategy and Authority? Do things flow more easily? Do relationships feel less draining? Do opportunities start coming to you without effort?

This is the experiment. You get to test how living in alignment with your design feels and see where life starts flowing more effortlessly. **Is it more satisfying** when you trust your inner process? **Does it feel like the current of life is taking you where you need to go**, instead of you constantly swimming upstream? That's what you're discovering through the practice of Human Design.

Think of it like tuning into your energy in the most authentic way possible. When you start following your Strategy and Authority, life begins to align. There's less resistance, more clarity, and greater fulfillment. It's about leaning into your natural rhythm and noticing the difference when you're operating in alignment versus when you're forcing something that doesn't fit.

A Blend of Ancient Wisdom and Modern Science

Human Design is both ancient and modern. It draws from over 28 years of empirical research, including charts from 8 million people. The system synthesizes insights from diverse fields, combining traditional knowledge like Western and Eastern Astrology, the I'Ching, the Hindu-Brahmin Chakra system, and the Kabbalah with modern scientific concepts such as **quantum mechanics**, **genetics**, and **biochemistry**.

The discovery of **neutrinos**—subatomic particles that carry information through the universe and imprint on our DNA—further anchors Human Design in a scientific framework. Neutrinos stream through us, influencing our energetic imprint at the exact moment of our birth, and help shape the BodyGraph. Once neutrinos were discovered to have mass and measurable influence, what once felt like a "belief system" became something more grounded in science. To me, the ability to measure these particles confirmed the legitimacy of the system as a practical, experiential framework for understanding life.

Human Design isn't about belief or theory—it's about experimentation. It offers a logical framework designed to be **tested** in real life. You'll discover how to manage your energy more effectively, make decisions aligned with your true nature, and navigate relationships and life challenges with greater ease and fulfillment. It's about reclaiming your authority over your life and recognizing where you've been conditioned to follow paths that aren't meant for you.

Reclaiming Your Authority

Ultimately, Human Design isn't about giving your power away to a chart or an expert. It's about **reclaiming your authority**. Your Strategy and Authority are the core tools that help you align with your true self. Everything else in the chart provides nuance, depth, and additional insight, but it's these two components that serve as the foundation of your alignment.

When you experiment with your Design and start living in accordance with your Strategy and Authority, you'll begin to see profound shifts in how life unfolds. Instead of constantly trying to force things to happen, you'll start to feel the natural flow of life carrying you toward your purpose.

3

Why Use Human Design?

Here's the question I hear all the time: *"But why should I use Human Design?"*

Because life is exhausting when you're living out of alignment.

Most of us spend decades trying to be what we're not—chasing jobs, relationships, diets, and lifestyles that look good on paper but feel terrible in our bodies. We're conditioned from childhood to measure up, fit in, and perform in ways that may have nothing to do with our true design. Human Design gives you a way to strip that conditioning back and return to what actually works for you.

Think of it like this: If you bought a car without an owner's manual, you'd spend years guessing—pouring the wrong fuel in the tank, using the wrong oil, driving it like it was built for speed when really it was designed for endurance. Eventually, it would break down. That's how most people live. Human Design is the manual that finally explains your model.

The Payoff of Living Your Design

- **Better Decision-Making**: No more second-guessing or outsourcing your choices. Strategy and Authority give you a reliable internal compass.
- **Healthier Relationships**: When you understand your aura type and how you interact with others, you stop taking things personally. You see mechanics at play, not flaws.
- **Energy Management**: Burnout happens when you push against your design. Human Design shows you where your energy is sustainable—and where it isn't.
- **Self-Acceptance**: Instead of wishing you were more like someone else, you begin to honor your uniqueness. Your quirks become features, not flaws.

Why It's Different from Other Systems

I've studied psychology at the doctoral level, explored coaching models, experimented with countless biohacking tools—and I can tell you this: Human Design is different.

It doesn't ask you to believe. It asks you to test. It's not about becoming something new; it's about unlearning what isn't you. And unlike personality tests that can shift with your mood or mindset, your design is fixed from birth. It's a consistent reference point you can return to anytime life feels confusing.

Why I Use It

For me, Human Design became the missing link between personal development and actual transformation. Therapy gave me insight. Coaching gave me tools. Biohacking gave me measurable results. But Human Design gave me *strategy*—a way to make choices that consistently led to less resistance and more flow.

It's not about living a perfect life. It's about living *your* life—

with clarity, alignment, and a hell of a lot less struggle.

4

What Is a Biohacker?

Before we dive further into my personal Human Design experiment, let's zoom out. You've probably heard the word *biohacking* thrown around on podcasts, Instagram reels, or at your local juice bar. But what does it actually mean—and how does it connect to Human Design?

At its core, biohacking is about taking conscious control of your biology. It's about making small, intentional shifts—whether in your environment, your nutrition, your sleep, or your mindset—that have an out-sized impact on your health and longevity. It's self-experimentation for the sake of optimization.

Some biohackers lean high-tech—think continuous glucose monitors, red light therapy panels, or $20,000 cryotherapy chambers. Others take a more minimalistic approach: fasting, cold showers, barefoot walking in nature. Both paths are valid, because biohacking isn't about gadgets—it's about results.

My Definition of Biohacking

For me, biohacking has always been personal. It's not about chasing immortality or becoming some Silicon Valley cyborg. It's about waking up every day feeling younger, clearer, and more aligned than I did yesterday. Although I do joke all the time saying I want to live to be 200 years old.

As a Doctor of Psychology, I was trained to study behavior and the mind. But through Human Design, I discovered that my biology—my actual cells—responded dramatically when I lived according to my energetic blueprint. That meant my version of biohacking couldn't just be about supplements and lab work; it had to include how I make decisions, how I use my energy, and even where I spend my time.

Why Biohacking Matters

Because aging is expensive. Not just financially—but emotionally, hormonally, and energetically. Every decision we make either accelerates the clock or helps us slow it down. By layering Human Design onto traditional biohacking, I found ways to:

- Reverse my biological age by over two years.
- Reclaim energy I thought was gone for good.
- Feel more grounded, confident, and resilient—not just physically, but psychologically as well.

This book is my road map to how I got there—and how you can, too.

5

Key Types of Biohacking

(For Informational Purposes Only — Not Medical Advice)

Biohacking spans a wide range of approaches, from nutrition and movement to cutting-edge genetic tools. Below is a general overview of the most common biohacking domains and how I've personally engaged with many of them throughout my journey.

Nutritional Biohacking & Nutrigenomics

Focus: Optimizing diet and nutrition to enhance health and cognitive function.

Includes: Supplements, intermittent fasting, dietary adjustments based on genetic insights, and metabolic tracking tools (e.g., Fitbit, Oura Ring).

My supplement routine is fairly structured. I typically take a few supplements first thing in the morning on an empty stomach. At lunchtime, I take a larger batch that needs to be consumed with food. Some supplements are reserved for specific days—just Monday, Wednesday, and Friday. Weekends tend to be lighter supplement days. At night, I take a few more before bed and a final pill right before falling asleep.

I don't have it down to a perfect science, and I'm not giving medical advice, but I've built this routine based on a combination of my DNA results, my nutritionist's guidance, and general recommendations for a woman in my age range. It's an evolving process, and I continue to adjust as I learn more about my body and its needs. (I'll go deeper into my coffee rituals and meat-eating preferences later in this book.)

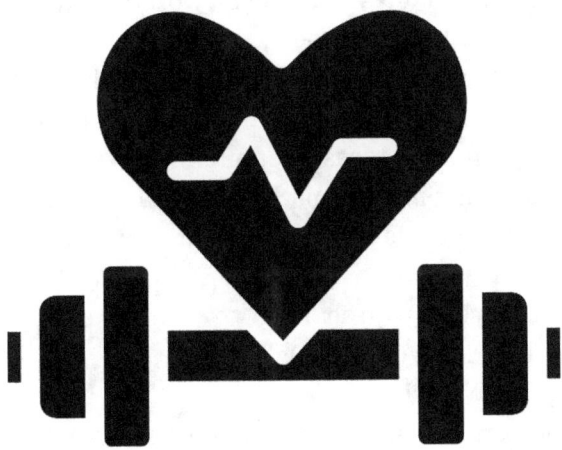

Exercise Biohacking

Focus: Maximizing physical fitness and recovery through innovative techniques.

Includes: High-intensity interval training (HIIT), wearable fitness devices, strength training, and recovery strategies.

As a woman focused on longevity and injury prevention—particularly falls that can lead to fractures—weight training is my top priority. I genuinely enjoy lifting weights, and research supports it as one of the best ways to maintain bone health. I'm not planning on falling and breaking anything, but let's be real: you hear those stories, and prevention matters. Ladies, it's time to lift.

While many younger women thrive in group fitness classes (which are great!), exercise routines should always reflect your individual age, health status, and goals. Personally, I aim for at least 30 minutes of cardio on workout days. I mix in swimming or biking for variety.

Due to a torn meniscus, I no longer walk, hike, or dance as much as I used to, but I still aim for 5–6 workout days per week. I do ab work at least that often. Free weights are my go-to, but sometimes the machines call to me. Something is always better than nothing. My current strength split is:

- Back & biceps (with abs)
- Chest & triceps (with abs)
- Leg day (with abs)
- Shoulders are sprinkled in with upper body as needed.

Peptides & Glycemic Control

Peptides have become a cornerstone of modern biohacking, especially for weight management, metabolic optimization, and glycemic regulation. Compounds such as Tirzepatide and Semaglutide (not "semiglutide") have gained massive attention for their ability to stabilize blood sugar, curb appetite, and support sustainable fat loss when used under medical supervision.

A next-generation compound, Retatrutide, remains in clinical trials and isn't publicly available yet — but early data has biohackers and longevity researchers buzzing. These agents can be powerful allies when used responsibly, but they are not casual supplements. Proper dosing, clinical monitoring, and integration with nutrition, sleep, and movement strategies remain essential.

The "There's a Peptide for That" Era

In the biohacking world, it's become almost a running joke: "There's a peptide for that." From muscle gain to mood, libido to longevity, the enthusiasm around peptides borders on wild-west territory. New compounding labs and online clinics seem to appear every 30 minutes, each claiming to have the latest cutting-edge protocol.

That excitement is understandable — peptides do show real potential — but it's critical to approach this space with discernment. These compounds can profoundly influence hormones, metabolism, and gene expression, and not all sources are reputable or regulated. Anyone experimenting with peptides should **work with a licensed provider**, verify purity and sourcing, and cross-check claims with current peer-reviewed research.

Peptides may very well shape the next decade of precision biohacking — but they're tools best handled with curiosity, caution, and evidence-based support. Once this book is out in the world, my next research rabbit hole will definitely be the peptide frontier. As of today, I'm not using any, but I'm endlessly curious — and I look forward to sharing whatever I discover with my community along the way.

Sleep Biohacking

Focus: Improving both the quality and duration of sleep.

Includes: Sleep tracking, optimizing the sleep environment, supplements, and restorative bedtime rituals.

At the moment, I'm mostly listening to my body and not relying on any sleep-tracking gadgets. (Although, if anyone's looking for birthday gift ideas — April 7th — a new Oura Ring wouldn't go unappreciated.) I do take a small handful of evening supplements and follow solid sleep hygiene practices, including all the usual suspects. My goal is to get a full nine hours each night, but realistically, my body settles somewhere between 7.5 and 8 hours these days.

Genetic & DIY Biology

Focus: Modifying genetic material or conducting personal biological experiments for enhancement.

Includes: CRISPR technology, blood testing, nootropics, implantable devices, and other self-experimentation tools.

Many biohackers go deep into these methods. Personally, I stick with regular blood testing and select nootropics. If you have the time, money, and curiosity to explore the rest, design your own plan—but know what you're getting into.

Mindfulness & Mental Biohacking

Focus: Enhancing cognitive performance and mental well-being.

Includes: Meditation, neurofeedback, mental health practices, exomind, theta chambers, binaural beats, hemispheric synchronization music, vibroacoustic chairs, crescendo audio beds, and more.

Mindfulness has been part of my adult life for years, but lately I've been experimenting more with **accessing flow states**. I've owned a NeuroAcoustic Sound Recliner for several years and am trained through the Center for Neuroacoustic Research, founded by Dr. Jeffrey Thompson (you may know him from the documentary *Heal*).

This chair has helped me train my brain to drop into theta brainwaves quickly—the brain's "healing state." Healing, in my view, is one of the most potent forms of biohacking. Over time, I developed a trauma unwiring protocol using this technology, inspired by EMDR but uniquely my own. Clients have experienced profound calm and clarity from it, and it remains one of my favorite modalities.

Wearable & Technology-Based Biohacking

Focus: Using technology to monitor and optimize health in real time.

Includes: Wearables that track metrics like heart rate, sleep, and stress levels.

I've intentionally broken my dependence on wearables and now enjoy relying more on my intuition. That said, as I mentioned earlier, I wouldn't turn down an Oura Ring.

One of my coaching clients recently took a break from his wearable because he became overly dependent on the numbers, similar to the anxiety many feel when stepping on the scale. Like all tools, wearables are best in moderation. They offer useful insights but should never override your **Inner**

Authority—a principle Human Design emphasizes deeply. Technology should be a tool, not a dictator.

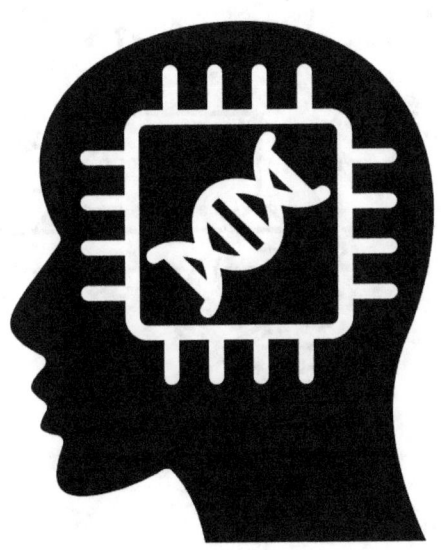

Transhumanism & Technological Enhancement

Focus: Integrating technology with human biology to enhance performance.

Includes: Genetic engineering, brain-computer interfaces, nanotech, and experiments like inserting microchips for data storage or receiving young blood transfusions.

I'm open-minded about these approaches, but for now, my focus is on tuning into my own biology rather than merging with machines.

Environmental Biohacking

Focus: Modifying surroundings to improve overall well-being.

Includes: Light therapy, air quality optimization, and intentional environmental design.

This was one of the biggest needle-movers in my biological age reversal (I'll go deeper in the Variables chapter). With seven of my nine Human Design centers open, I'm especially sensitive to my surroundings.

In February 2025, my city launched a Blue Zones Ignite study to evaluate its walk-ability, food access, public spaces, and community programs. I didn't move here for that reason—I relocated in 2023—but learning about the study felt like confirmation that my environment was supporting my longevity goals in ways I hadn't fully realized.

Social Biohacking

Focus: Improving social and emotional well-being.

Healthy human connection is one of the most powerful anti-aging tools available. When I realized my social circle in LA wasn't fulfilling, I made a major life pivot: I moved to Miami. That shift rejuvenated my spirit, expanded my opportunities, and, I believe, positively impacted my biology.

Later in this book, I share more about the emotional and

psychological "cool sh*t" I did to heal—changes that became a cornerstone of my biohacking journey. For more on why social connection matters so much for well-being, check out this great overview: *Social Connectedness* – ScienceDirect.

6

Why Human Design Matters for Biohacking

Most biohacking advice is one-size-fits-all. But biology isn't generic—it's personal. What works wonders for one person might burn another out. That's where Human Design comes in.

Your **Strategy** and **Authority**—the foundation of Human Design—are decision-making tools that align you with your biology. For me, following my Projector strategy (waiting for the invitation) and Ego Authority (making decisions from my willpower center) changed everything.

Here's why it matters for biohacking:

Better decisions = better biology. Every choice you make — what to eat, when to rest, who to spend time with — impacts your body. Alignment leads to more energy, faster recovery, and slower aging.

You might be shocked at how good it feels to be truly aligned — and equally shocked to realize how long you've been unconsciously settling for misalignment. Many people believe they're already doing "the best they can" because they pride themselves on their past choices and the intention behind them. But in my experience, it wasn't until I tried some new strategies — based on my Human Design chart — that I discovered I *could* feel even better, more energized, and more myself.

I had to humble myself and stay open to experimenting with different decision-making strategies. When I did, I was stunned by how quickly I felt the shift — and how much misalignment I had been tolerating as my "normal."

Openness teaches wisdom. Our undefined centers are where we absorb outside energy. When unmanaged, they can create stress, burnout, and even accelerate aging. But when we learn to work with them, they become our greatest teachers.

This isn't just about awareness — it's about making friends with our shadow sides, laughing at our own patterns, and cultivating patience with our process. Growth isn't linear, and the more we can meet ourselves with compassion, the more freedom and vitality we unlock.

Precision protocols. Of all the tools I've tried, **Environment** and **Digestion** (the Variables in Human Design) gave me some of the biggest breakthroughs in reversing my biological age.

I'll admit — I underestimated these at first. They require a deeper level of self-awareness, and honestly, the results feel almost too subtle to measure at first. But once I leaned in, got my exact time of birth, and started experimenting, these Variables turned my biohacking from generic to *couture*.

They helped me make choices that felt tailor-made for my body, and those choices created compounding results — better sleep, better labs, better energy — and a younger biological age.

In short: Human Design gave me a personalized biohacking roadmap. Instead of guessing what might work, I could test and track based on my chart.

*Before we dive deeper into strategies, authorities, and centers, let's zoom out. Human Design starts with your **Type**—your overall energetic role in life. There are five types, each with its own aura, gifts, and challenges. Understanding them is the first key to unlocking your design.*

II

Types, Auras & The Projector Life

7

The A.A.A.A. Process

After more than eight years of experimenting with Human Design and biohacking, I've come to realize that much of this journey — and life itself — is about cultivating awareness and asking the right questions.

The one I return to most often is:

Is this something I can accept, or is it something I need to adapt to?

That simple question echoes the essence of the Serenity Prayer, which has always deeply resonated with me:

"Grant me the serenity to accept the things I cannot change, courage to change the things I can, and the wisdom to know the difference."

Human Design has become my modern lens for living out that timeless wisdom. It's shown me how to live as myself — how to understand my energy, make decisions correctly, and work with the conditioning field instead of against it.

But Human Design isn't just about knowing your chart. It's about **living it.**

You have to experiment.

You have to see how it plays out in real life.

That process — the lived experience — has allowed me to peel back layer after layer of societal conditioning and step more fully into my true self.

This approach has become my compass. It has guided me through romantic relationships, major career pivots, health scares (including the humbling moment when my biological age tested *older* than my chronological age), spiritual awakenings, and the general chaos of modern life — with more clarity, confidence, and grace.

It's also made me into a kind of spiritual warrior — someone who can meet uncertainty with inner strength and resilience.

Honestly, I believe the more life kicks our butts, the more we all become warriors. It's just part of the deal.

As I share later in this book, I even pursued stand-up comedy for two solid years — and not just locally. I performed in two countries, facing down fear night after night. That chapter of my life became a living laboratory for this process. Comedy was the ultimate form of adaptation and action — and let me tell you, it involved a *sh*t-ton* of experimentation, failure, and getting back up again.

What I learned is this: transformation isn't about piling on more hacks or doing life perfectly. It's about cycling through four simple but powerful stages:

Awareness

Notice what's happening — in your body, your energy, and your environment. Without awareness, you stay stuck in autopilot, repeating conditioned patterns.

Awareness is the first step in both Human Design and biohacking: learning to actually see and feel what's *real* for you. For Projectors (like me), this step is a life-saver because our aura pulls in so much from others. Without a pause, we can get tangled up in someone else's energy before we even realize it.

The AAAA Process gives you a built-in grounding cord — a way to anchor back into yourself before you make a move.

Acceptance

Once you become aware, the temptation is to fight it — to resist what you find. But resistance burns energy.

Acceptance doesn't mean you approve of everything. It means you stop pretending things are different than they are.

Human Design taught me to accept my open centers, my need for rest as a Projector, and my sensitivity to environment.

Acceptance brings peace. It clears the mental noise so you can hear your own inner authority and make choices from a place of alignment.

Adaptation

Life never stops throwing curve balls. Adaptation is about staying flexible and agile without losing yourself.

This is where Strategy and Authority become your compass, guiding you to shift, experiment, and respond intelligently. For me, adaptation looked like changing my eating schedule to honor my Indirect Light digestion, adjusting my sleep environment, and choosing co-working spaces that aligned with my Internal Markets environment.

Adaptation is where you get to test what works for *you* — not just what works in theory.

Action

Nothing changes until you move.

But action only works when it's aligned. This isn't about hustling harder or forcing outcomes. It's about taking intentional steps once you've checked in with your body, your awareness, and your authority.

Aligned action is the biohack that integrates it all — it's what makes change real.

Why It Matters

This four-part process — **Awareness, Acceptance, Adaptation, Action** — has been my compass through every major season of my life: career pivots, health crises, relationship chaos, and identity shifts.

It ties Human Design directly into the world of biohacking by giving you a repeatable cycle you can run every single time you want to change something in your life.

Every teaching chapter that follows — on Aura, Strategy, Authority, Signature, Environment, Digestion, open centers, and deconditioning — fits into this framework:

- **Awareness** of what drains or supports you
- **Acceptance** of your mechanics and sensitivities
- **Adaptation** through experimentation and trial-and-error
- **Action** that moves you forward, younger, lighter, and more aligned

This is the framework that will keep showing up throughout the book — your built-in compass for hacking aging and living fully as yourself.

8

The Four Types & Their Auras

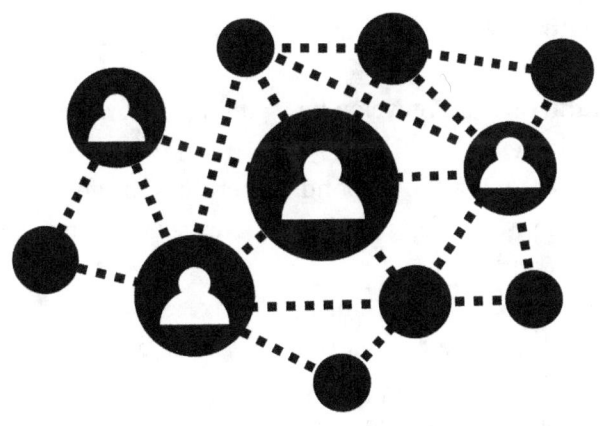

Human Design begins with your **Type**—the broadest layer of the system. Type describes how your energy is designed to move in the world, how your aura communicates before you say a word, and the most natural way for you to find flow in life.

There are four Types (five categories, with Manifesting Generators included as a Generator sub-Type): **Generators, Manifesting Generators, Projectors, Manifestors, and Reflectors.**

Each has:

- A distinct **aura** (how energy is exchanged with others),
- A **strategy** (how to engage with life),
- A **signature** (the feeling of alignment),
- A **not-self theme** (the red flag of resistance).

Generators (about 37% of the population)

- **Aura:** Open and enveloping—pulling life toward them like a magnet.
- **Strategy:** Wait to respond. Generators thrive when they notice what life presents and answer with their gut or inner authority.
- **Signature:** Satisfaction.
- **Not-Self Theme:** Frustration.

Generators are the true builders of the world. They are designed for mastery through repetition and devotion to what excites them. Their sustainable energy becomes powerful when directed toward work or activities they genuinely love. But when they say "yes" out of obligation, burnout quickly follows.

* *My observation:* In coaching, I've seen Generators redis-cover their vitality simply by asking themselves, will this give me more satisfaction or more frustration? It looks so simple, but it changes everything.

Manifesting Generators (about 33% of the population)

- **Aura:** Open and enveloping (like Generators).
- **Strategy:** Wait to respond, then inform before acting.
- **Signature:** Satisfaction.
- **Not-Self Theme:** Frustration.

Manifesting Generators (MGs) are dynamic, multi-passionate, and non-linear. They often skip steps, pivot quickly, and hold many interests at once. This isn't inconsistency—it's correct for them. They are designed to move fast and to change course as needed.

* *Practical Lesson:* Many MGs I've worked with struggle with guilt over "quitting" projects. But once they understand that their design is meant to pivot quickly, the guilt dissolves — and their energy gets freed up for what truly lights them up.

MGs thrive on efficiency. If they abandon a project, it's not failure — it's usually because they've discovered a faster, better, or more efficient way forward.

Projectors (about 21% of the population — that's me)

- **Aura:** Focused and penetrating—zeroing in on the other person.
- **Strategy:** Wait for recognition and invitation.

- **Signature:** Success.
- **Not-Self Theme:** Bitterness.

Projectors are the guides. In business they are Advisors. Their energy is not built for endless work but for seeing how others can use their energy more effectively. Their penetrating aura gives them a unique perspective—but only when their wisdom is recognized and invited.

   * *My own biohack:* As a Projector, one of the biggest shifts for me was resting more and waiting for genuine invitations. When I stopped pushing like a Generator and started honoring recognition, my biological age began to reverse. Don't worry my fellow Projectors, we are going to take a deep dive into what it's like to be a Projector later in this book. I would never want to trigger your bitterness, after I just told you to "wait" for an invitation. I got you.

Manifestors (about 8–9% of the population)

- **Aura:** Closed and repelling—it pushes outward, creating independence and impact.
- **Strategy:** Inform before acting.
- **Signature:** Peace.
- **Not-Self Theme:** Anger.

Manifestors are initiators who impact. They're here to start things, spark movements, and catalyze others. Their power is in beginning, not sustaining. Because their aura is closed, people often feel left out, so informing is vital to reduce resistance.

   * *Practical note:* Manifestors often calm their environment—

and themselves—when they simply say, "Here's what I'm doing." It removes resistance and allows them to move freely and experience what they want, which is usually peace.

Reflectors (about 1% of the population)

- **Aura:** Sampling and resistant—it absorbs, mirrors, and reflects.
- **Strategy:** Wait a full lunar cycle (about 28 days) before making big decisions.
- **Signature:** Surprise.
- **Not-Self Theme:** Disappointment.

Reflectors are the mirrors of humanity. They show the health of their community and environment through their own experience. Because they have no consistent energy centers, they are deeply conditioned by the spaces and people around them.

Lesson from a friend: One of my closest friends is a Reflector. Watching how quickly her health and mood change based on her environment taught me just how literal Human Design can be. With Reflectors, the "where" is everything. They may not admit this but from watching them they seem to be the most patient people on the planet.

Why This Matters

Your **Type** is the foundation of Human Design. Your **Aura** is how others experience you, instantly and unconsciously. Together, they set the stage for how to approach life through your Strategy and how to avoid the resistance of the not-self.

When you honor your Type, life gets easier. Invitations

appear for Projectors, satisfaction grows for Generators, peace returns for Manifestors, and Reflectors find themselves in the right places with the right people to enjoy more surprises.

That's the starting point for Human Design as a biohacking tool: knowing your Type and Aura mechanics, and experimenting with how they actually feel in real life.

9

Auras: Beyond The Walls

Why Your Sleep (and Desk) Might Be Affected By More Than Just Noise

In Human Design, the aura is everything. It's one of the ways we connect, envelop, sample, absorb, repel, and get conditioned by the world around us.

This is especially relevant when it comes to **sleep**—but it also applies to how we **work,** who we share space with, and why you might feel exhausted after sitting next to someone all day (even if you barely spoke).

Let's dive into how auras operate, how they penetrate physical barriers (yes, even walls), and why that might be impacting your rest, recovery, and energy throughout the day.

Aura Mechanics 101:

Each Human Design type has a unique aura:

- **Generators & MGs** – *Open and enveloping* (they welcome others in, can also envelop others' energy)
- **Projectors** – *Focused and absorbing* (think: laser beam,

penetrating)
- **Manifestors** – *Closed and repelling* (like a club speaker— projecting energy outward whether you like it or not)
- **Reflectors** – *Sampling* (they taste and mirror the energy around them)

These energetic fields don't stop at your skin. They don't even stop at walls.

Auras extend outward, and depending on the person's design, can interact with others—even through drywall, lumber or glass. Its my best guess that an Aura is 6 feet and the other persons Aura is 6 feet, I think that some people can sense Aura's 12 feet away.

Aura Penetration Is Real:

I know it sounds wild, but **auras can go through walls**.

So if you've ever felt "off" while trying to sleep or concentrate—even when you're physically alone—you might not *actually* be alone in your energetic space.

Projector auras, for example, are deeply focused and absorbing.

That's wonderful for reading someone in a 1:1 session, but terrible if you're trying to fall asleep and the neighbor's Sacral energy is humming through the wall behind your bed.

Same goes for desks and work-spaces. If you're a non-energy type (especially Projectors & Reflectors) spending hours in an open office or even working side-by-side with a Generator friend at a cafe, *you're in their field*.

And if you have open centers (especially Sacral, Solar Plexus, or Head), you're probably amplifying their stuff *and* thinking it's yours. So don't call your therapist just yet, that sensation you're feeling probably isn't yours. If you want to double check that it's not yours, get out of their aura for 30-90 minutes and you'll probably feel like yourself again, and saved that money you were going to spend on an extra therapy session.

Sleep + Walls = Hidden Conditioning

Let's talk about **bed placement**.

If your bed shares a wall with the neighbor's bedroom, their kitchen, or a child's playroom; you could be spending your nights soaking in someone else's energy field.

I know that sounds like Feng Shui heresy, but I'll say it:

Move your bed.

Try sleeping in a part of the room where no wall is shared.

If possible, keep your sleeping zone *at least 6 feet away* from anyone else's aura—even if they're in a separate apartment.

Yes, even **pets** have auras. If your sleep is suffering, kick the dog (or the cat or the parrot) out of your bedroom and run the experiment.

I love my alone time during sleep. And no, it's not because I snore (though that's the excuse I usually give). It's because I can't sleep deeply when I'm in someone else's energy. And if you're a Projector or another non-Sacral type, you probably can't either, or as deeply as you wish.

Why Sleep Alone? (Especially for Non-Sacral Types)

Sleep is when our aura naturally is itself —when we clear out all the external energy we've absorbed during the day.

For **non-Sacral beings** (especially Projectors & Reflectors), it's crucial to sleep **alone** whenever possible.

Here's why:

- You don't have a defined Sacral Center, so you're more sensitive to the *buzz* of people who do (Generators & MGs).
- Sharing a bed can feel overstimulating.
- Even *being near someone* in the next room can throw off your natural rhythm.

Sleep hygiene isn't just about light and temperature—it's about *energetic space.*

Workspaces Matter, Too

This isn't just about sleep — it's about how you spend your *awake* hours, too.

If you sit next to someone for multiple hours a day — at a shared desk, in a co-working space, or even at your kitchen table — you're not just sharing air. You're sharing **auras.**

This matters most for non-energy types and those with open centers, because you're taking in far more than just conversation.

So if you've ever caught yourself thinking:

"Why am I so exhausted after working near that person?"

...it's probably the **aura**, not your to-do list.

On the flip side, if you're a non-energy type and you actually *want* to borrow a little buzz, sitting next to a Generator can be a fun, temporary hack. It's not technically "using" them — you're not huffing their fumes or jumper-cabling yourself to their motor — but you *will* get a boost.

They won't notice a thing... and hey, sometimes that's

exactly the little energy lift you need to finish this damn book. It's actually a version of using the AAAA Process we just mentioned above.

Biohacking With Aura Awareness

If this sounds "extra," good. This is a **biohacking book**, and sleep and recovery are foundational to anti-aging, hormone regulation, mood, and cellular repair.

Assess *everything* that might be aging you or disrupting your body's natural cycles.

Aura boundaries are real—and most of us are totally un-aware of them.

This isn't about being a diva. It's about being precise.

You're worth the experiment.

Reclaim your space. Reclaim your sleep. Reclaim your energy.

Where do you have the energy to exercise?

The sacral center in Human Design is a vital source of life force energy, associated with creativity, sexuality, and generative energy. It reflects the body's response to satisfaction and its instinctual reactions, manifesting through the "yes" and "no" responses that guide individuals toward their correctness or correct decision making. When the sacral center is defined and functioning optimally, it provides a constant flow of energy for work, play, and relationships, fueling their life with enthusiasm, make babies and vitality.

In addition to the sacral center, Human Design features three other motors: the root center, the solar plexus, and the heart center. The root center serves as a pressure center, providing adrenaline and drive to initiate action and cope with stressors, thus propelling individuals forward. The solar plexus is linked to emotional energy, driving awareness of feelings and intuition, ultimately influencing decision-making processes. The heart center, also known as the will center, embodies the energy of willpower, ego, and material resources, motivating individuals to pursue their desires and manifest personal goals. Each motor plays a distinct role in guiding energy flow, emotional responses, and decision-making in the Human Design system.

Every person can exercise, even if their chart doesn't contain one of the four motor centers. But speaking personally—as a Projector, which is considered a non-energy type in the Human Design system—people with a defined Sacral center seem to have energy all day long and often don't need a nap, unlike me.

Sacral energy needs to be fully burned off for them to feel satisfied and sleep deeply. It's like a cell phone battery: if a Sacral person takes a nap, it's basically like recharging the battery mid-day—meaning they'll need to do even more to drain it before bed. That's why some Sacral folks can nap *and* sleep well—they've simply figured out how to burn through their energy reserves. (Unless they're relying on sleeping pills or benzos, but that's a different conversation.)

I work out more days than not, but I rest less between sets when lifting weights because I know my energy is limited. My cardio is zone 2 cycling for 30 minutes—I've given up long walks and retired from jogging years ago. When I did run a half marathon, my Generator sister was right beside me. I swear I was snorting her energy just to cross the finish line.

In my workshops, I often use the metaphor, "I'm jumper

cabling onto a Generator's battery." Similarly, if I go out dancing at a club at night, I know I'm riding the energy waves of all the Generators in the room (they make up 70% of the population, after all). I often don't realize how tired I am until I step out of their auras—then it hits me: "OMG, I'm exhausted." Goodnight.

How Can Non-Energy Types Work Out?

Manifestors, Projectors, and Reflectors might prefer less energy-intensive exercises or shorter workouts due to their unique energy dynamics in Human Design.

Manifestors often enjoy workouts that are quick and impactful. They may prefer high-intensity intervals or time-efficient routines that allow them to engage their energy without feeling drained. (*especially when exercising alone, outside of anyone else's aura*)

Reflectors, as mirrors of their environment, may find that their energy fluctuates significantly. They might enjoy spontaneous, short bursts of movement rather than structured exercise—opting for activities like light stretching or dancing, depending on their mood. (*especially when exercising alone, outside of anyone else's aura*)

In contrast, **Generators** have a sustainable energy source and often thrive on longer, more vigorous workouts like running or weightlifting. Their defined Sacral center allows them to tap into and sustain energy more effectively. They may spend more time at the gym, have conversations, not rush through a workout but not necessarily burn more calories.

Generators and Manifesting Generators, in Human Design, possess a specific energy dynamic that makes activities like running marathons not only possible but often enjoyable. Generators have a defined Sacral center, providing a consistent source of life-force energy that can be harnessed through activities they love—giving them endurance and satisfaction in movement.

Manifesting Generators share this Sacral energy but also bring the ability to move quickly and pivot between tasks. They often prefer efficient, varied routines—think bursts of high-intensity mixed with steady-state training. Remember: MGs love efficiency and are built for nonlinear progress. Let them switch things up as needed, even if that means skipping steps or changing direction mid-workout.

Matching exercise modalities to each type can enhance

physical wellness by aligning workouts with natural energy rhythms. For **Generators**, prolonged activities like long-distance running or cycling work well—as long as they're passionate about the activity. For **Manifesting Generators**, variety is key: a mix of intensity levels and movement styles keeps them engaged and energized without feeling boxed in.

Projectors, in Human Design, are known for their ability to focus deeply and absorb the energy of those around them — thanks to their undefined centers. When we're in the presence of Generators, especially during group workouts or classes, we can inadvertently ride the Generator energy wave. This isn't always conscious; it's an energetic effect.

You might push past your natural limits or feel unstoppable in the moment, only to crash later. (This is exactly like the example I gave earlier — me at the club, vibing off everyone else's sacral energy until I suddenly realized, *"OMG I'm exhausted,"* and had to go home.)

Having many open or undefined centers means we're more receptive to the energetic dynamics around us. In a gym filled with active, energy-producing bodies, this can lead to over stimulation — or even a temporary loss of inner alignment. We can find ourselves moving in ways that reflect other people's rhythms rather than staying true to our own. (But there are some Projectors who have a lot of their centers defined so this may not apply to you so completely)

This distinction took me a while to really figure out. I couldn't understand why I never got into the group-fitness craze — or the "sweat-pals / class pass" trend where people love meeting up to exercise together. I'll occasionally join a group class, but honestly, I'm usually there more for the *other* biohack: the socializing that happens afterward. The class itself tends to feel more draining than energizing.

Personally, I've learned to experiment with timing and environment to make exercise work for me. When I go to the gym, I'm very aware that I'm surrounded by Generators — just by law of averages. I choose the slowest time of day so I can borrow just enough Generator energy to lift weights and feel productive, but I avoid peak hours. Too many Generators in one place can be overstimulating and exhausting, especially if I have to wait for equipment or share machines.

I've found there's a sweet spot — a "just right" number of people in the room — that helps me feel focused and motivated without getting overwhelmed. When I hit that sweet spot, I leave feeling accomplished and clear-headed rather than depleted.

It's the same with swimming. I enjoy having other people in the pool area — there's something about their presence that feels energizing — but I can't share a lane when I'm doing laps. Having my own lane allows me to stay in my own flow and really honor my rhythm without being pulled into anyone else's pace.

Projectors thrive with shorter, intentional workouts that emphasize recovery and quality over quantity — especially when done outside of anyone else's aura. This is when we can truly honor our own energy, rather than amplifying or depleting it by accident.

Learning this balance has been key for me. It's an ongoing experiment — adjusting my workout times, choosing when to be around other people, and noticing how my body feels afterward. This trial-and-error process is how Projectors (and really, all non-energy types) can create a relationship with movement that supports rather than drains them.

10

I Am Not a Generator

One of the biggest "aha" moments in my Human Design journey was realizing, without a shadow of a doubt, that I am **not** a Generator.

This may sound obvious if you've seen my chart, but for decades, I lived as if I was one. I forced myself into Generator habits, Generator work hours, and Generator expectations. I even measured my worth by how much I could "do" in a day.

The problem? As a Projector, that approach slowly ground me down. It was like driving a sports car on the wrong kind of fuel — eventually the engine starts knocking.

The Generator Myth I Bought Into

I grew up in a culture obsessed with hustle. If you weren't working 10-hour days, juggling a side gig, and still somehow making time to meal prep, train for a marathon, and learn Mandarin, you were "falling behind." (Sarcasm intended)

And let's be real — Generators (and Manifesting Generators) can make that lifestyle look effortless. They have the sacral battery to fuel long hours of output, as long as they enjoy what they're doing. They thrive on responding to life and building momentum through action.

I, on the other hand, was barely hanging on. Even when I matched their pace, it came with an invisible price tag: burnout, brain fog, and eventually, resentment.

Why This Realization Changed Everything

When I finally embraced that I am not a Generator, I stopped making myself wrong for needing rest. I stopped feeling guilty for working in focused bursts instead of marathon sessions.

More importantly, I started **using** my Projector gift: seeing things others can't. My value wasn't in keeping up with the herd — it was in noticing patterns, offering guidance, and creating strategies that saved everyone time and energy. (If they invited me, of course)

And here's the kicker: once I stopped trying to "do it all," my results actually improved. I was more impactful, not less.

Famous Generators: Dalai Lama, Albert Einstein, Carl Gustav Jung, Mozart, Madame Curie, Luciano Pavarotti, Dustin Hoffman, Greta Garbo, Madonna, Elvis Presley, Walt Disney, Anthony Perkins, Dolly Parton, Mel Gibson, Meryl Streep, Eddie Murphy, Robin Williams, Celine Dion, Garrison Keillor, Ram Dass, Kreskin, Johnny Carson, Oprah Winfrey, Ellen DeGeneres, Paul Simon, Truman Capote.

Famous Manifesting Generators: Mother Teresa, Vincent van Gogh, Friedrich Nietzsche, Alois Alzheimer, Marie Antoinette, Mata Hari, Kate Winslet, Bruce Lee, Charlie Chaplin, Bill Cosby, Barry Manilow, Donald Trump, Tom Hanks, Elton John, Billy Joel, Liza Minelli, Angelina Jolie, Nicole Kidman, Arlo Guthrie, Sidney Poitier, Gwyneth Paltrow, Lily Tomlin, John Denver, Hilary Clinton

The Biohacking Connection

This is where the Human Design + biohacking fusion really shines. Most mainstream health advice is aimed at the majority — and in Human Design terms, that means the Generator types who make up 70% of the population.

So if you're not a Generator, you have to be *very* selective about which advice you take. That "30-minute morning HIIT session before work" may be perfect for a Generator but totally unsustainable for a Projector.

By recognizing I wasn't a Generator, I finally stopped trying to biohack in ways that didn't suit my energy mechanics. Instead, I focused on:

- Short, impactful workouts followed by real recovery.
- Making my environment work for me so I didn't have to "push" all the time.
- Timing my decisions and actions in a way that leveraged my natural focus and invitations.

Knowing what I am not opened the door to understanding the other types, too. And if I'm not a Generator... I'm definitely not a Manifestor either. But I had to bump into that wall, too, before I learned the lesson.

11

I Am Not a Manifestor

If realizing I wasn't a Generator was a relief, realizing I wasn't a Manifestor was... humbling.

Manifestors have this aura of pure autonomy. They're the fire-starters, the initiators. When they get an idea, they can just act on it — no permission, no warm-up period, no waiting for the stars to align. They move first, and the rest of us catch up.

That instant ability to begin manifesting? I admired it. I envied it. And for years, I tried to imitate it, as I think many of us do before we discover our Human Design type.

My Manifestor Phase

There was a time I would *force* myself to "just do it," thinking that if I acted decisively enough, I could create momentum like a Manifestor. After all, I read the book "Just Do It," which was inspired by the Nike slogan, from cover to cover in my twenties.

I'd launch projects without invitations.

I'd send out pitches before anyone asked for them.

I'd jump into "initiating mode" without checking in with my authority.

And on a rare occasion... it worked. But more often than not, I'd end up exhausted, bitter, or wondering why no one seemed as excited about my "big idea" as I was.

The Manifestor Difference

Here's the thing: Manifestors are designed to initiate — it's literally their gift. They have a motor connected to their throat center, which allows them to move ideas into reality with almost shocking speed and ease.

Projectors like me? We don't have that same motorized connection. If I try to push things into motion without being recognized or invited, it's like forcing a door open that was meant to swing on its own. Sure, I can shove it — but it's awkward, it creaks, and the hinges resent me for it. After all no-one like a wedding crasher.

Famous Manifestors: Johannes Kepler, Helmut Kohl, Elisabeth Kubler-Ross, Krishnamurti, Hermann Hesse, Jack Nicholson, Bruce Springsteen, Mao Tse-tung, Jesse Jackson, Maya Angelou, Art Garfunkel, Tracey Ulman, Marth Stewart, Tommy Smothers, George Carlin, Ra Uru Hu, Robert De Niro, Bob Newhart, Jennifer Aniston, Susan Sarandon, Tim Robbins, George W. Bush

Biohacking Through Non-Initiation

This realization didn't just change how I worked — it changed how I *biohacked.*

When you know you're not here to initiate, you can let go of the constant cortisol spike that comes from trying to "make things happen." My biology calmed down when I stopped picking fights with my own design. (On a side note, I do have the 25-51 channel, which is the channel of initiation. It's too deep to go into for the purposes of this book. But if you were to schedule an individual session with me because you also have the 25-51 channel, I can better explain to you how this works and how it works differently than Manifestor.)

Now, I wait for invitations before diving into big projects — and I conserve my energy for what truly matters. That's biohacking at its finest: doing less, gaining more.

If I'm not a Generator and I'm not a Manifestor, what else could I be? Spoiler: I'm definitely not a Reflector either — but understanding why taught me more important lessons in my Human Design experiment.

12

I Am Not a Reflector

If I once envied the sustainable energy of Generators and the initiating power of Manifestors, my feelings toward Reflectors were... different.

Reflectors are rare — only about 1% of the population — and their charts are completely open. No defined centers at all. They are the ultimate chameleons, constantly reflecting the energy of the environment and the people around them.

Why I Knew I Wasn't One

I may have seven open centers, but I still have definition. I have one channel — my one little fixed bridge in a sea of openness. And let me tell you, even with just that, I still know what it's like to get *knocked around* energetically.

If I were completely open, like a Reflector, I think I'd have either joined a monastery or fled to a remote cabin in the woods by now. Reflectors are incredibly sensitive — and their decision-making process is tied to the lunar cycle. They need 28 full days to process big decisions.

Me? I have Ego Authority. Twenty-eight days? I can barely wait 28 hours before I'm ready to make a move if it feels right.

Someone once posed a really good question to me. They visually looked at my chart and asked, "What is it like to be only one channel away from being a reflector?" As if I could somehow magically have a sense of what being a reflector was like because I was like a second cousin, but there is no way for me to answer that question because definition changes everything in a chart, even if it is only one channel. Be careful not to make assumptions. It was a good question and I did have to ponder it for a while.

Reflector Magic

Even though I'm not one, I deeply admire Reflectors. When they're in the right environment, they're like living mirrors — showing people the truth of who they are just by existing. But if the environment is wrong? It's like watching a flower wilt in fast-forward.

This is why I stress environment so much in my work. You don't have to be a Reflector for your surroundings to make or break your energy.

Famous Reflectors: Rosalyn Carter, Eduard Morike, Thorwald Dethlefsen, Ammachi, Scott Hamilton, Dick Smothers, Fyodor Dostoyevsky, Sandra Bullock, Richard Burton, H.G. Wells, Yul Bryner, James Frey

The Reflector Biohack

What I've learned from Reflectors is this: the more open you are, the more important it is to curate your environment with intention.

For me, that means being ruthless about where I live, who I spend time with, and the energy I allow into my space. Every open center is an entry point for conditioning — but also for wisdom. The trick is knowing the difference and choosing wisely.

So if I'm not a Generator, not a Manifestor, and not a Reflector... what am I? That's where the truth — and the transformation — began.

13

To Be a Projector

At the BG5 Business Institute, Projectors are referred to as **Advisors**.

In other Human Design circles, we go by many names: Guide, Teacher, Consultant, Counselor, Oracle, Shaman, Priestess, Professor.

The common thread? We're here to **guide**. To **see**. To **illuminate**.

We're not here to do all the heavy lifting—we're here to show others how to lift better.

Discovering I was a Projector was like finding the missing page of my life manual — the page that explained why I'd been running myself into the ground trying to keep up with everyone else. Before Human Design, I thought my exhaustion was a personal failing. I believed I just wasn't disciplined enough, strong enough, or "motivated" enough to keep the same pace as everyone else. So I pushed harder, over committed, and burned out... then wondered why I couldn't sustain it.

Then my chart told me the truth: I'm a Projector. I'm not designed to generate my own endless energy. I'm here to **guide**, not **grind**.

What Being a Projector Really Means

Projectors make up about 20% of the population. We have a focused and penetrating aura that's designed to see deeply into others — their patterns, their potential, their possibilities. But here's the catch: that superpower only works when we're **recognized and invited** to share it.

Without the right invitation, our insights can come across

as intrusive or unwanted. And when we try to initiate without being asked, it's like swimming upstream — exhausting and frustrating. Think of it like showing up to someone's birthday party when you weren't invited, talking a little too much, and realizing people are starting to gossip. Awkward.

The Invitation Rule

Learning to **wait for invitations** was one of the hardest — and most liberating — lessons of my life.

It's not passive. It's not about sitting on the couch eating bonbons until someone knocks on your door. It's about using the waiting time to take care of yourself, study your craft, and live so fully that when the invitation comes, you're ready.

Another way to think about it is this: when someone truly recognizes you and invites you in, they're also giving their **consent**. It's like they're voluntarily putting on a seatbelt — preparing themselves, opening their eyes and ears, and signaling that they're ready to receive your guidance.

That moment of recognition creates an experience that's beautiful, powerful, and absolutely worth the wait.

It's also about discernment. Not every invitation is worth accepting. With my **Ego Authority** (more on this in the next section), I had to learn to ask:

- Do I actually want this?
- Does this feel / taste like a yummy invitation?
- Will this bring me joy, pride, and success?

The Burnout Trap

Before I understood my design, I lived like a Generator wannabe — filling my schedule, saying yes to everything, and thinking "busy" meant "successful." But Projector energy doesn't work that way.

When we overdo it, **bitterness creeps in**. And for Projectors, bitterness is the red flag waving furiously in the wind. It's our body's way of saying, "You're out of alignment."

Now, I see **rest not as laziness but as fuel**. Downtime is what allows me to show up sharp, clear, and impactful when it's time to guide. Our gift lies in seeing into others, spotting inefficiencies, and helping Generators—whose strategy is to respond—use their energy in more aligned and sustainable ways. Coaching Manifestors to inform before they act and Advising Reflectors to be patient and see what decision comes to them after a lunar cycle.

Understanding Our Energy

Projectors must be especially mindful of how we use our energy. We recharge slowly. And because our auras are designed to absorb and focus, we're naturally sensitive to the world around us. That makes us incredible at reading people—but also vulnerable to **burnout and identity confusion** if we're not careful.

Let's be honest: the modern world is built for Generators.

Social media, productivity hacks, even 9-to-5 work culture—all designed for people who can sustain energy throughout the day. So when you're scrolling and suddenly feel like you should be doing more? Pause. That message probably isn't for you.

You're not broken. You're just not the energetic majority.

The Cost of Being Unaware

When we forget our nature, we go into survival mode:

Over-committed. Under-rested. Hustling for recognition that doesn't align.

It's a straight shot to burnout.

Bitterness sets in — not as a loud outburst, but as a quiet corrosion.

When I remember who I am, I give myself grace. I rest when I need to. I work in focused bursts. And I remind myself, again and again, that I don't have to follow the world's pace.

Yes, I may need more downtime than others.

No, that doesn't make me weak. It makes me wise.

The Hidden Gift: Efficiency

Here's one of the coolest side effects of being a Projector in a Generator world: we become **efficiency experts** — out of necessity.

Because we can't rely on endless energy, we've learned how to get the most out of short windows of productivity. We often accomplish in **90 minutes** what others take three or four hours to do.

The wild part? We rarely give ourselves credit for it. Many Projectors don't even realize how effective they are. We've adapted to a world that wasn't designed for us—and we're good at it. That's worth celebrating.

A Different Perspective: The Time Factor

Generators have energy that stretches throughout the day — 8, 10, even 12 hours of output.

Projectors? We get a few solid hours. That's it. And that's enough.

If I get a couple 90 focused minutes of quality work in a day, that may be my entire energetic output. After that, I might need a nap, a walk, or quiet time to study whatever interests me.

That's not laziness. That's alignment.

Celebrating Our Wins

As Projectors, we often skip the part where we celebrate. We go from task to task, forgetting to pause and acknowledge what we've accomplished.

But when I stop and think, *Wow, I just completed that thing in record time*, I feel successful. And that's our **signature** — our home frequency.

Once I taste that, I can enjoy the rest of my day without guilt or pressure to do more.

Final Thoughts: Embrace Your Projector Power

If you're a Projector, let this be your reminder:

You're not here to operate like everyone else. And that's a very good thing.

Honor your need for rest.

Recognize your unique rhythm.

Be selective with your energy.

Wait for the invitations that feel delicious — the ones that light you up and make you feel truly seen. And when they come, check in with your Authority before saying yes.

The more you honor your energy, the more often you'll experience that sweet, satisfying sense of **success**.

And that, my friend, is what being a Projector is all about.

Famous Projectors: JayZ, Michael Jackson, Marilyn Monroe, Taylor Swift, Brad Pitt, Serena Williams, Dennis Rodman, John F Kennedy, Sir Winston Churchill, Gigi Hadid, Emma Watson, Jodie Foster, Gerald Butler, Halle Berry, Whoopi Goldberg, Mick Jagger, Kiera Knightly, Jackie Chan, Kayne West, Steven Spielberg, Princess Diana, Denzel Washington, Charles Darwin, Osho, Woody Allen, Elizabeth Taylor, Lance Armstrong, Queen Elizabeth II, Nelson Mandela, Leonardo DiCaprio, Freddie Mercury, Abraham Lincoln, Jeff Bezos, Wayne Dyer, Arianna Huffington

Why This Matters for Biohacking

If you're a Projector — the traditional "hustle culture" approach to health optimization can backfire. We can't biohack our way into being a Generator. But we *can* design our lifestyle, our environment, and our habits in ways that make our natural energy work for us, not against us.

I stopped chasing other people's blueprints and started building my own. That's when the real transformation began — not just in my energy, but in my biological age.

Once I finally understood what it means to be a Projector, I had a big question:

"Okay... now what?"

Knowing my type gave me validation — but it didn't give me a game plan. Human Design doesn't just stop at telling you *who* you are; it shows you *how* to navigate life without burning out.

And that's where **Strategy** comes in. Strategy is the "how." It's your personal user manual for moving through the world with less resistance and more flow.

For Projectors like me, Strategy was what saved me from pushing, forcing, and working myself into exhaustion.

But before we dive into how to use it, let's talk about one of the most underrated Projector biohacks that makes Strategy even easier to follow: ***the art of the nap.***

14

Nap time: The Secret Weapon of Projectors and Maybe You Too

Being a Projector isn't just about waiting for invitations — it's about respecting your body's need for more rest. If you're a Projector, naps aren't optional; they're medicine. And even if you're not a Projector, learning how to optimize sleep is one of the most effective biohacks you can implement right now.

Before we dive into Strategy, let's talk about rest. Because if your energy isn't being renewed consistently, no amount of correct decision-making will keep you from running yourself into the ground.

General Biohacking Sleep Tips

These 10 strategies are foundational for optimizing sleep and overall energy renewal:

1. **Consistent Sleep Schedule** – Go to bed and wake up at the same time every day to stabilize your circadian rhythm.
2. **Create a Sleep-Inducing Environment** – Dark, cool, and quiet. Blackout curtains and an eye mask can be game-changers.
3. **Limit Blue Light** – Shut down screens early or wear blue-light-blocking glasses in the evening.
4. **Nervous System Reset** – Breathwork, meditation, or gentle yoga before bed can help you downshift.
5. **Targeted Supplements** – Magnesium, melatonin, L-theanine, and valerian root can support deep sleep (but check with your doctor first).
6. **Gratitude Journaling** – Clear mental clutter with 3 minutes of reflection before bed.
7. **Cut Caffeine & Alcohol** – Both disrupt deep sleep. Stop caffeine at least 6–8 hours before bedtime. I do not judge people who enjoy their cocktails, but true biohackers do

eventually give up alcohol all together, just an FYI

8. **Daily Movement** – Regular exercise supports quality sleep, but avoid HIIT right before bed. (There are some exceptions to this, for example myself, due to the my variables, which is a huge section coming up later in this book)

9. **Power Naps** – Keep them under 30 minutes (unless your body needs more) and avoid late-afternoon naps, specifically Generators. Projectors do what you want, just listen to your body. I often do a 40-60 minute nap, more days than not.

10. **Track & Adjust** – Devices like the Oura Ring, Fitbits or Whoop can reveal patterns and help you fine-tune your routine.

Human Design Sleep by Type
Generators & Manifesting Generators (Energy Types)
Generators wake up like a fully charged iPhone. They need to use up that energy before bed or sleep can be restless.

- If you're still buzzing at night, move your body — even a short walk or chore helps discharge excess energy.
- For kids, bedtime routines that include movement (yes, even play!) can help them settle. Generator kids may not benefit from rigid bedtime schedules. They sleep best when they're naturally tired. Rituals can help—my sister and her husband do this with my niece every night. Some think this revs kids up. For Generators, it helps them discharge energy in a healthy way.
- Naps are fine as long as they don't prevent you from burning through your "battery" by night.

Projectors

Here's a hot topic: sleeping with other people. Our focused, absorbing aura doesn't turn off at

night. When you share a bed, you're in someone else's energy field for hours — and that matters, especially for Projectors. This isn't being high-maintenance. It's energetic hygiene.

If you're a Projector and you value deep, rejuvenating rest— consider sleeping alone. Yes, I've used my snoring as an excuse to avoid sharing hotel rooms on vacation. But the real reason isn't my snore; it's that I cannot sleep well in someone else's aura, especially if it's humming with Sacral energy. Projectors need more rest than most—we don't have a Sacral motor to keep us running all day.

Begin winding down at least an hour before bed. Let your body and mind decompress. Afternoon naps aren't lazy— they're medicine. Your focused aura stays "on" while you sleep, so when you can, carve out time to rest alone (or create a reset space away from others' energy).

Honestly, my dream sleep setup is extreme but specific: no cats, no dogs, no fish, and definitely no people within 12 feet of me. That may sound dramatic, but when I get that kind of uncontaminated rest, everything changes. My recovery is deeper, my clarity returns, and I'm kinder to myself the next day.

If we're dating, we can absolutely negotiate sleeping arrangements. Want morning sex? Great. I'll come to your room after I've slept deeply and feel rested — and trust me, the sex will be better that way. If you're worried that means we'll never sleep together, we can figure out compromises. But be real: if someone can't handle your sleep needs, they might not be the right match for you.

Bottom line: sleeping and napping are not indulgence for Projectors — they're essential. Treat your rest like a non-negotiable biohack. Your body, your energy, and yes—your relationships—will thank you.

Manifestors

Manifestors are non-energy types too, so they also need recovery. Their only "rule" is to inform the people around them if they need space, a nap, or a late-night walk — it creates peace and reduces resistance. Their Aura is closed so they'll sleep with who, what or whenever they want.

Reflectors

Reflectors do best with an early bedtime (10 PM if possible) and a gentle evening routine that clears energetic residue. Naps are usually beneficial for recalibrating their system.

A Day in the Life of a Non-Energy Projector (Me)

Here's how this plays out for me:

- Wake up naturally around 8:00 a.m.
- Morning ritual: brain-fuel coffee + 90 minutes of focused work.
- Light lunch + supplements, then **nap #1** (40–60 min, blackout curtains).
- Afternoon: client sessions or co-working with a Generator friend (while secretly running on her energy).
- Evening: weightlifting, protein refuel, social time, then two dinners (because vampire digestion is real).
- Bedtime: food in stomach, nighttime supplements, deep

restorative sleep.

Final Thoughts

Sleep is when your body repairs, your mind recalibrates, and your cells literally get younger. For Projectors, rest is our secret weapon — our way to stay vibrant, clear, and effective guides.

So before we move on to Strategy, give yourself permission to rest. Your body — and your bio-age — will thank you.

15

The Pendulums of Each Human Design Type

In Human Design, we often reference **eight key emotional states** that correspond to each Type. These aren't just abstract concepts—they're *signatures* that indicate alignment (or misalignment) with your design.

When you're living in alignment, you'll experience:

- **Satisfaction** (Generators)
- **Success** (Projectors)
- **Peace** (Manifestors)
- **Surprise** (Reflectors)

On the flip side, when you're out of alignment, you may feel:

- **Frustration** (Generators)
- **Bitterness** (Projectors)
- **Anger** (Manifestors)
- **Disappointment** (Reflectors)

These emotional states serve as an *energetic barometer* for whether you're living true to your design or engaging in patterns that pull you off track.

As I often say in my workshops:

- Generators, when you feel **satisfaction**,
- Projectors, when you feel **success**,
- Manifestors, when you feel **peace**,
- Reflectors, when you feel **surprise**,

...it's a clear sign you're in the *right place*, at the *right time*, with the *right people*, creating more of that aligned state.

The opposite is also true:

- If Generators are feeling **frustrated**,
- Projectors are feeling **bitter**,
- Manifestors are feeling **angry**,
- Reflectors are feeling **disappointed**,

...it's a signal that you're in the *wrong place*, at the *wrong time*, with the *wrong people*—and that continuing down that path will only amplify the misalignment.

Until you fully understand and experiment with your **Inner Authority**, these emotional states act like a **pendulum**—swinging you between alignment and misalignment. The goal isn't perfection; it's to spend *more time* in satisfaction, success, peace, and surprise, and *less time* in frustration, bitterness, anger, and disappointment.

You can use these keynotes as **quick decision-making guides** for simple, everyday choices. But when it comes to bigger decisions that require more time, energy, commitment, or focus, you'll want to rely on your **Inner Authority**—which we'll explore in the next section.

III

Strategy, Authority, Profiles & Living Your Design

16

Strategy: Your Compass for Flow

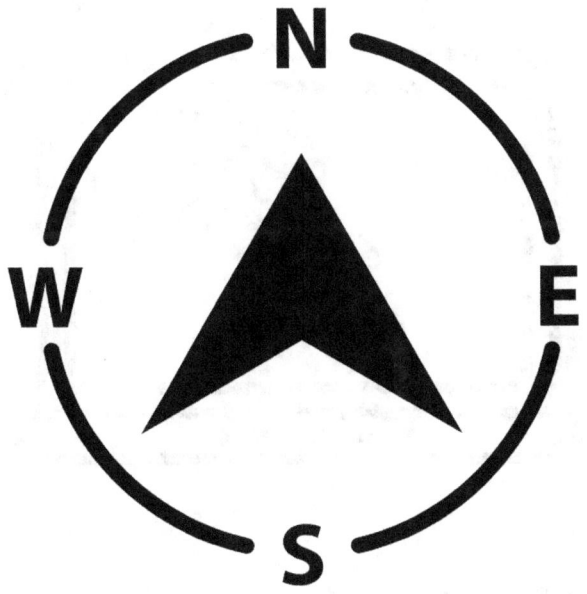

If Type is the foundation of Human Design, **Strategy** is the compass. It's the practical tool for how to approach life in a way that puts you in the right situations, with the right people, at the right time.

Every Type has its own Strategy. Following it doesn't guarantee a perfect life, but it dramatically reduces resistance. It's how we enter into correct experiences and align with our Type's **signature feeling**—the state of being that tells us we're on track.

Generator & Manifesting Generator Strategy: (Wait) to Respond

Generators are not designed to initiate. Their power comes from responding to what life brings—people, opportunities, even small decisions. The sacral "yes" or "no" tells them whether something is correct, in general, we'll get more specific with Inner Authority in the next section.

- When they follow this: They feel deep **satisfaction**.
- When they don't: They get stuck in **frustration**.
- *Practical takeaway:* Instead of chasing, Generators thrive when they pause and let life give them something to respond to. That's when their energy is sustainable and ready to build something really satisfying.

Projector Strategy: Wait for (Recognition and) Invitation

Projectors are guides, not workers. Their gift is in seeing others clearly, but that wisdom only lands when it's invited. Their Strategy is to wait until they are **recognized and invited** before offering their perspective.

- When they follow this: They feel **success**.
- When they don't: They slip into **bitterness**.
- *Practical takeaway:* Recognition is the key. A Projector's guidance only works when it's seen and welcomed. Waiting isn't passive—it's how Projectors conserve energy and make the right connections and end up in the right opportunities.

Manifestor Strategy: To Inform (Before Acting)

Manifestors are initiators. Their energy is here to start things, create movements, and open doors. But their closed aura can feel abrupt or repelling to others if they don't **inform first**.

- When they follow this: They experience **peace**.
- When they don't: They trigger **anger**—in themselves (and potentially others).
- *Practical takeaway:* A simple "Here's what I'm doing" goes a long way. Informing reduces resistance and allows Manifestors to move freely without creating unnecessary

friction and anger.

Reflector Strategy: Wait a Lunar Cycle

Reflectors are deeply tied to the rhythm of the moon. Their Strategy is to wait a full **28-day lunar cycle** before making major decisions, so they can see how they feel in different energies and environments.

- When they follow this: They find **surprise** in life's unfolding.
- When they don't: They fall into **disappointment**.

* Practical takeaway: For Reflectors, patience is power. Time gives them clarity, perspective, and alignment.

Why Strategy Matters

Following your Strategy is an experiment. It may feel unnatural at first because most of us have been conditioned to operate differently. But when you begin to test it, you'll notice patterns: less resistance, more flow, and a sense that life is "meeting you" instead of you pushing against it.

Strategy is how we enter into life correctly. It's not about controlling outcomes—it's about entering into the experiences that are correct for us, which then unfold into growth, relationships, and opportunities that support who we truly are.

In Human Design, you may hear people talk about the term **"fractal."** Think of it like sacred geometry — a natural pattern that unfolds with beauty and precision. For me, Strategy is the entrance point into that natural flow of life, the place where alignment begins to reveal itself.

It's like watching petals of a rose slowly open, or a school of fish gliding together in perfect formation, or a flock of birds shifting in sync across the sky. That's the rhythm of life when you're aligned.

When you follow your Strategy, you're in your correct fractal. And the magic is this: when you encounter someone else who is also living authentically by their Strategy, you instantly recognize, *we're on the same fractal.*

17

Inner Authority: Your Built In Decision Maker

In Human Design, **Inner Authority** is your internal decision-making compass. If Strategy is how you approach life, Authority is how you know when to say yes, when to say no, and when to wait.

It doesn't come from the mind. It comes from the body. Not logic. Not pros-and-cons lists. Not asking five friends for their opinion. Your Authority is unique to your chart, and when you honor it, you're guided into aligned choices that support your vitality and flow.

When you ignore it? Resistance builds. Stress rises. Your biology pays the price.

The Seven Inner Authorities

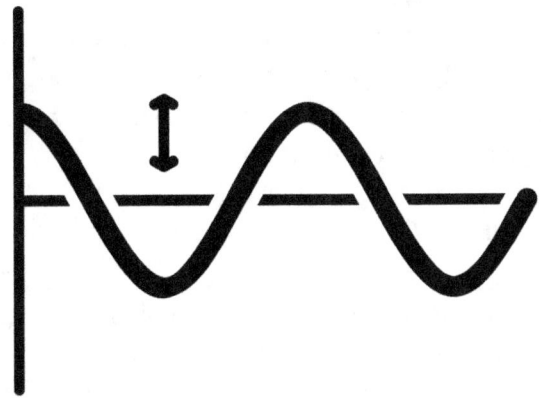

Emotional Authority (Solar Plexus)

- **Population**: ~47–50% (most common)
- Emotional Authority is the most common Authority in Human Design, and it's rooted in the Solar Plexus center. Unlike other Authorities, the Solar Plexus doesn't operate in real time. Instead, it moves in emotional waves — sometimes high, sometimes low, sometimes somewhere in between.

This means one of the golden rules for Emotional Authority is: **there is no truth in the now.**
You're not designed to make big decisions in the heat of a

euphoric high, nor in the depths of a low. Clarity comes only after the wave has been felt and has settled.

Key to Decision-Making

Wait for the emotional waters to calm. Rash choices made at the peaks or valleys of your wave often lead to frustration, disappointment, anger, or bitterness — the not-self signatures that tell you you've veered off track.

Practical Tips

- **Sleep on it.** Give yourself at least 24 hours (and sometimes longer) to ride out the wave.
- **Surf before you decide.** As I say in my workshops, you need to feel the crest and the crash before you can trust the stillness.
- **Use placeholders.** Pencil it in, play it by ear, or say, *"I'll circle back before the deadline."* This gives you the time to find neutrality.
- **Shop smart.** I often joke in my workshops: *"I know some of you have clothes in your closet with the tags still on them."* (Cue the emotional authority folks nodding or laughing in agreement.) To avoid impulse buys at the high end of the wave, leave your wallet at home and go back later if you still want it. For Amazon shoppers, put items in your cart but don't click *purchase* until the next day. You'll be surprised how often you delete half the cart — and laugh at yourself for almost buying all that stuff.

The Biohacking Connection

Emotional Authority isn't just about better choices — it's

about biology, too. Rushing into decisions at the peak of a high can spike cortisol, while choosing from the low end of the wave can mimic depressive thought patterns. Both put stress on the body and accelerate aging.

Waiting, on the other hand, regulates your nervous system. It allows your hormones to settle, your body to find balance, and your mind to reconnect with clarity. In biohacking terms, you're building emotional resilience — which directly supports longevity.

Decision Rule

Wait for emotional neutrality before making decisions. When the answer feels calm, grounded, and steady — not euphoric, not despairing — that's your green light to move forward.

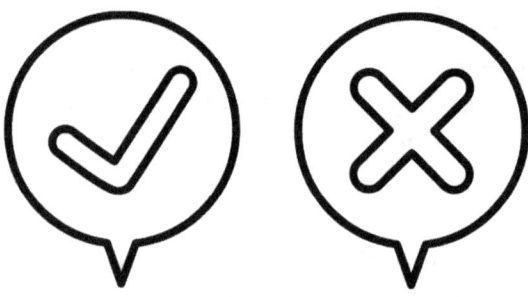

Sacral Authority

- **Population**: ~35% (Generators & Manifesting Generators)

The Sacral center is your gut's "yes" or "no" system. It speaks in simple, clear sounds or body reactions—*uh-huh* (yes) or *uh-uh* (no). If there isn't clear quick response then the question might need to be asked again later or asked in a different way. As I say in my workshops, multiple choice questions are challenging for this authority. In school many of our exams were multiple choice, and in my opinion people with Sacral authority are probably smarter than the score they received on the exam. If a quiz or exam was True or False style, Sacral authority people probably did extremely well.

You're designed to respond to life as it presents itself. It's not about initiating—it's about noticing what response is happening *in the moment.*

Key to decision-making:

Listen to your gut. It knows. Your sacral response will tell you whether something is correct for you or not.

Practical tip:

Don't think—*feel.* Watch for physical responses or subtle vocalizations when someone asks you a yes/no question. You don't need to explain your sacral truth. You just need to honor it.

* **Biohacking Connection**: Sacral beings can waste huge amounts of energy pushing through obligations. Trusting the sacral response prevents burnout and preserves energy for true satisfaction.

Splenic Authority

· **Population**: ~11%

The Spleen is the oldest awareness center in the body—connected to survival, health, and instinct. If this is your Authority, it means decisions come as quick, intuitive hits—fleeting sensations, subtle nudges, or an inner whisper. From the Splenic authority clients that I've spoken with, most of them describe the sensation as a sound, but whatever it is, listen to it.

These signals don't repeat themselves, so trust in the *first* knowing is essential.

Key to decision-making:

If it feels instantly right (or wrong), *listen.* The splenic hit is quiet, but accurate. Miss it, and the moment might be gone.

Practical tip:

Start noticing your instincts—those micro-moments where you just *know.* It might be a chill, a tightening in the chest, or a deep sense of ease. Don't over-analyze. It's subtle but reliable.

* **Biohacking Connection**: Splenic clarity often guides people toward health-preserving choices—like avoiding a food, supplement, or person. Trusting it can be the difference between resilience and illness.

Mental Projectors (Environment / No Inner Authority)

- **Population**: ~3.5%
- No inner compass—clarity comes by speaking in the right environment.
- **Decision Rule**: Talk it out in the right space.
- **Practical Tip**: Surround yourself with supportive listeners and places that feel good.

* **Biohacking Connection**: The *where* is as important as the *what.* A wrong environment or wrong sounding board creates static. Mental Projectors literally "think clearer" in the right room.

Self-Projected Authority (G Center)

- **Population**: ~2.8% (only in Projectors)

If you have Self-Projected Authority, your truth is in your voice. It emerges when you speak *from the self* —from identity, direction, and core values. I love working with this authority and I often know how to coax out of this authority the answers they seek. Sometimes I've simply taken notes and if they don't hear the answer immediately after they vocalized it, I will read back the notes to them. These are my clients who really appreciate that I understand how this works because other life coaches can talk too much and not really listen with a curious mind. These people are really wise they need support more than your guidance. It's more like, hey Dr Julie, help me get the answers that are inside of me that I can't seem to access alone.

It's not about advice—it's about *being heard.* What you say when no one interrupts is where your clarity lives.

Key to decision-making:

Speak your truth out loud. You'll know it when you hear yourself say it.

Practical tip:

Talk to someone who listens well—without fixing or advising. Or record yourself and listen back. Your voice will lead you home.

* **Biohacking Connection**: For these individuals, clarity = coherence. When they hear themselves, their nervous system relaxes. This isn't about advice; it's about self-recognition.

Reflectors (Lunar Authority)

- **Population**: ~1.4%
- No consistent inner compass. Must wait a full lunar cycle.
- **Decision Rule**: Slow down. Clarity is found in time.
- **Practical Tip**: Journal and notice patterns across the 28-day cycle.

* **Biohacking Connection**: Reflectors thrive when they give themselves time. Acting too soon mimics chronic stress states. Waiting restores alignment and protects their health.

Ego Authority (Will/Heart Center)

Population: ~1% (exclusive to some Manifestors and a very small number of Projectors)

Ego Authority, also known as Will Center Authority or Heart Center Authority, is one of the rarest decision-making strategies in Human Design. It's not about waiting for emotions to settle (like Emotional Authority) or relying on intuition (like Splenic Authority). Instead, Ego Authority is direct and driven by desire, willpower, and what you're genuinely motivated to commit your energy toward.

Key to Decision-Making:

Ask yourself: *Do I actually want this?* If the answer isn't a full-bodied yes, then it's a no. Trust me—talking it out loud can make your answer obvious. For example, earlier today, I had a well-intentioned salesperson pitch to me. I got off the call, and without thinking, I muttered, "Oh hell no." I was surprised by how clear my reaction was, but that's the power of Ego Authority.

Practical Tip:

Pay attention to what naturally comes out of your mouth or body in the moment. If you hear yourself saying, "I'll do it" with genuine conviction, that's alignment. But if you hesitate, second-guess, or feel pressure to prove yourself, that's a sign to step back.

Note from me: As someone with Ego Authority, I've learned that honoring my desires isn't selfish—it's essential. When my heart is behind something, my energy follows. When it isn't, I burn out or get bitter.

Why Inner Authority Matters

Every decision you make impacts your biology—who you spend time with, where you live, when you eat, and what you commit to. When you follow your Inner Authority, you stop simply "thinking" your way through life and start letting your body lead. That's the ultimate biohack: stress lowers, vitality rises, and life feels more like flow than force.

As a female, I used to rely too heavily on emotions to guide my decisions. But when I learned to tune into my unique Inner Authority, I still honored my feelings but stopped letting them take the lead. I discovered that my Ego Authority was the turning point. I stopped trying to prove myself and started listening to my will. If my heart wasn't in it, it was a no. That simple shift reversed years of burnout—and yes, it even showed up in my biological age tests as I regained youth.

Final Thoughts on Authority

Authority isn't mental—it's somatic, embodied, and lived. When you honor your Authority, your life begins to align in ways that logic could never orchestrate.

Living with Ego Authority has been one of the most radical shifts in my biohacking journey. My willpower doesn't negotiate. If I say it, it's real. If I don't, it isn't. Trusting this, rather than resisting it, has been the key to aligning with my truth.

Strategy and Authority are the ultimate biohacks. They sync your decisions with your biology, your energy, and your truth. And as I've shown throughout this book—when I honor mine, I literally get younger.

18

Ego Authority in Practice: A Projector's View

So, what's it like to be a Projector with Ego Authority?

In a word: *rare.*

Ego Authority is less than 1% of the population, and if we're talking about Ego Projected Authority specifically, that number drops to around 0.834%. The only other Type that can have Ego Authority is the Manifestor.

When I first discovered this, it felt like someone had handed me a VIP pass to my own life. But as with any VIP pass, there were rules to follow.

What Ego Authority Really Means:

In Human Design, your Authority is your decision-making GPS. For me, decisions don't come from my mind (which is too easily influenced by others) or my emotions (which rise and fall like waves). Instead, my decisions come from my Ego Center—the Will Center.

Here's how it works for me:

- *Do I actually want this?*
- *Will it bring me pride or success?*
- *Is this worth the commitment of my energy, time, and heart?*

If the answer isn't a resounding yes, then it's a no.

The Invitation + Desire Formula

As a Projector, I still need to wait for recognition and invitation. But even once the invitation comes, I need to check in with my desire. If it doesn't feel like a heart-centered yes, or if I don't feel the *will* to commit to what the invitation requires, then it's not for me.

This has taught me to say "no" more often—even to "good"

opportunities—because if I don't want it, it'll drain me. And when I'm drained, I can't guide anyone effectively.

The Challenge of Ego Authority

Living with Ego Authority isn't always easy. Society doesn't always appreciate people who lead with the question, "What's in it for me?" But the truth is, if I'm not fully behind something, my energy won't sustain it. Forcing myself to do something just because it's expected? That leads to burnout, bitterness, or illness.

For example, a girlfriend asked me to go for coffee, and my Will Center said no. The quick "no" felt like a mini relief. However, when I received an invitation to go to Bulgaria in January (in the snow) for a Human Design conference, my Will Center said yes—and I felt excited.

The energy it would cost me, the money it would cost me, the time it would cost me weren't calculated by my Will Center in terms of quantity. It's as if my body knew which decision would benefit me and likely be a win-win for everyone involved. The coffee with my friend would have felt like work, and I'm fairly certain she has Munchhausen syndrome—so she would have been draining me. On the other hand, Bulgaria, though cold, dark, and snowy in the winter, came at the perfect time—right after a trip to England I had already planned. My jet lag wouldn't be too bad transitioning from UK time to Bulgaria time, and I'd actually be able to focus and absorb the knowledge at the conference.

I gained so much from that experience, and many of the lessons will be shared intermittently throughout this book. Trusting my not-so-logical Will Center has been a fun and interesting ride, and I can't wait to see what happens next.

Honestly, writing a book had to come from this center, because logically, after the pain of writing my doctoral dissertation—and having trauma from the nuns in Catholic school who would yell at me and make me stay inside during recess to do my homework—writing is not something I enjoy. It had to be my Will Center at work, and this book must serve a bigger purpose. It's for all of you because my "mind" definitely did not want to write a book.

Ego Authority taught me that self-honoring isn't selfish— it's essential. When I'm aligned with what I truly want, I bring my full power and heart to everything I do. Everyone benefits when I honor my will.

The Biohacking Link

Once I began applying Ego Authority to my biohacking practices, everything accelerated. I stopped doing protocols because I "should" and only committed to the ones I genuinely desired:

- **Intermittent fasting** (because I wanted to feel light and sharp)
- **Weightlifting** (because it made me feel powerful)
- Skipping that **cold plunge** (because let's be real—I didn't want to do that!)

Applying my Ego Authority wasn't just a game-changer for my health—it shifted my entire approach to biohacking.

Just when I thought I'd uncovered all there was to know about Human Design, my Profile added a whole new layer of insight. Two numbers revealed not just my learning style and challenges, but also how I truly relate to the world. It was like discovering a whole new dimension to how I function and interact. It was the final piece of the puzzle—making sense of my personal design in a deeper way.

19

Living Your Lines: The 12 Profiles

If Human Design Type is your operating system, and Inner Authority is your decision-making GPS, then your **Profile** is the role you're meant to play in the story of your life.

Profiles are built from two numbers — one conscious (the first number, what you're aware of) and one unconscious (the second number, how others see you). Together, these two lines describe your learning style, your personality, and how you connect and interact with the world around you.

Profiles aren't personality tests. They're not about boxes you fit into, but about patterns you'll recognize in how your life naturally unfolds. Understanding your Profile brings clarity to why you operate the way you do, why you approach relationships the way you do, and how your lessons in life are meant to be lived.

After more than eight years of experimenting, I've also come to think of the Profile as a kind of **costume** you wear — one you didn't consciously choose. It's part of how people perceive you, how they judge you, and how they label you. It's the version of you that shows up in the outside world before you even get to explain yourself. That's why we often say Profile makes up about 70% of your personality. It's not your whole essence, but it's the closest description we have of what it feels like to live out your lines.

Now that I understand the themes of my Profile, I walk into a room differently. I know people are probably judging me. I know they're labeling me. I know they already think certain things about me — and that's okay. It's innate in us to look for patterns to feel safe in the world. I accept it fully. I come back to the AAAA Process we talked about earlier — Awareness, Acceptance, Adaptation, and Action — and I anchor myself there.

Instead of resisting the judgment or trying to reshape how people see me, I lean into my Profile and let it guide me toward my signature. For me, as a Projector, that signature is success. For others, it's satisfaction, peace, or surprise.

And here's the beautiful part: when I live this way, I can love people unconditionally, hold compassion for myself, and even get excited about showing up authentically — without fear. Life feels lighter, more playful, and far more enjoyable when I embrace the role I was designed to play.

1/3 – "One Three Profile" — Investigator / Martyr

Deep diver + experimenter. You build a rock-solid foundation through research and then learn by bumping into life. Expect trial-and-error as part of your growth.

1/4 – "One Four Profile" — Investigator / Opportunist

The 1st line builds a strong foundation through study and research. The unconscious 4th line waits for the right opportunity to externalize that foundation, influencing through personal connections and networks. Relationships are everything for you.

2/4 – "Two Four Profile" — Hermit / Opportunist

The 2nd line carries natural gifts that others see before they do. They need to be called out. The 4th line builds influence through community and opportunity.

2/5 – "Two Five Profile" — Hermit / Heretic

This is a projected profile—people see potential in them and project expectations. The 2nd line prefers retreat, while the

5th line draws attention and must use discernment to deliver practical solutions. Discernment is key.

3/5 – "Three Five Profile" — Martyr / Heretic

The 3rd line learns through trial and error—experimenting, bumping into life, and adapting. The 5th line adds a universalizing quality, able to turn lessons into solutions others can apply. This profile is resilient, adaptable, and often carries a "hero" or "problem-solver" projection.

- **Case Study: Living as a 3/5**
- I'm a 3/5 myself, and life as this profile feels like running a giant experiment. I've failed forward more times than I can count—but every "mistake" gave me data I could use. Over the years, I've crashed through comedy sets, diet fads, and relationship blowups, only to walk away with lessons that later became wisdom. My 3rd line is constantly experimenting. My 5th line draws people who expect me to have the answer. The balance is honoring my Ego Authority so I only step into roles I *want*—otherwise, the projection field can backfire. This Profile explains why my biohacking has been so hands-on: I test it all, keep what works, and share what's worth repeating — which is exactly why this book exists.

3/6 – "Three Six Profile" — Martyr / Role Model

This Profile begins with trial and error (3rd line) and matures into the wisdom of the 6th line Role Model. The journey unfolds in stages: experimenting, retreating, then embodying lived wisdom and inspiring others.

4/1 – "Four One Profile" — Opportunist / Investigator

The 4th line influences through its network, while the 1st line establishes a stable foundation of knowledge. This Profile often has a fixed destiny and is meant to impact people within their community.

4/6 – "Four Six Profile" — Opportunist / Role Model

The 4th line thrives on relationships, while the 6th line matures through three phases: trial-and-error youth, withdrawal in midlife, and eventual embodiment as a Role Model.

5/1 – "Five One Profile" — Heretic / Investigator

Highly projected upon, 5/1s are expected to deliver solutions. The 5th line universalizes wisdom, but to do that effectively, it must be grounded in the 1st line's strong foundation.

5/2 – "Five Two Profile" — Heretic / Hermit

This Profile carries both projection and retreat. The 2nd line hides, but the 5th line pulls attention. When called out correctly, they can deliver transformative insights to the collective.

6/2 – "Six Two Profile" — Role Model / Hermit

The 6th line undergoes its three-phase process (experiment, retreat, embody). Combined with the 2nd line's natural talents, this Profile often becomes a wise and trusted example to others later in life.

6/3 – "Six Three Profile" — Role Model / Martyr

This is one of the most complex Profiles, beginning with a chaotic 3/3 phase before gradually maturing into a Role Model.

Even later in life, the unconscious 3rd line keeps pulling them into trial-and-error, making for a dynamic but sometimes turbulent path.

Why Profile Matters

Profile is less about what you do in the moment and more about your **relationship with life itself — and with other people.** It shapes how you learn, how you connect, how you stumble and recover, and even how others perceive and respond to you.

One of the easiest ways I've found to explain Profile is through a **workplace analogy.** Imagine I were running the Human Resources department of a large corporation. Each Profile represents a different kind of role someone might naturally thrive in. Just as a company looks for specific talents, skills, and abilities to fill different departments, Human Design Profiles reveal the "job description" your birth chart is already wired for.

This is why I'd love to assist corporations in the future by actually running their employees' Human Design charts. By matching people's Profiles to their work roles, companies could see massive benefits:

- Fewer mental health breaks and burnout days
- Less absenteeism from employees who feel disengaged
- More job fulfillment and satisfaction across the board
- Stronger personality-career alignment

In other words, instead of relying on self-report personality tests (which can be biased or easily gamed), Human Design Profiles cut straight to the truth of how someone is designed to operate.

Profiles explain so much of what we observe in life but can't always put into words. They clarify why some people seem to "fail forward" and learn best through trial and error, why others need to retreat before they're ready to share, and why certain individuals seem to carry an aura of responsibility they never consciously signed up for. Profiles don't just describe behavior — they reveal life's recurring patterns and help you stop resisting them.

When you begin to live your Profile consciously, life feels less like stumbling through chaos and more like fulfilling a role in a script that was written for you all along. It's not about limitation; it's about recognition.

And just when you start to think Profiles are nothing more than numbers on a page, they come alive the moment you begin watching them play out in real time. Take it from me: life with a **3/5 Profile** is anything but a spectator sport. It's messy, experimental, unpredictable, and endlessly instructive. But it's also rich, alive, and deeply aligned with the role I came here to play.

20

3/5 Projector Deep Dive

So, what's it like to have a 3/5 profile in Human Design? What does it mean?

It's a mix of being a martyr, a heretic, a messenger, and someone who learns through trial and error. Think about the scientific method: I learn by doing, by experimenting, by bumping into things—and yeah, spilling the milk. It's a messy, nonlinear process I know all too well.

But let's be real: being a 3/5 Projector—especially with seven open centers—can stir up some deep, unrelenting **bitterness**. The bitterness of constantly hitting walls, tripping over invisible wires, and fumbling your way through life like it's one giant spiritual gymnasium. Growth is earned. And often? It's earned through pain. (Ouch ouch ouch.)

Sometimes that bitterness just sits there, simmering, ready to explode. It's not easy. But over time, I've come to accept that it's part of my design. This is the hand I was dealt when I landed on Earth, and I don't get to redraw the cards. Sure, it builds resilience. But do I wish I had a choice in the matter?

Absolutely.

I don't know what it's like to have any other profile. This is my ride: this chart, this Profile, this Projector body with Ego Authority. And this 3/5 life? Holy Schnickies. It's not easy. But it's mine.

The 3: Trial and Error, Baby

The "3" in my profile is the experiential one. The experimenter. The one who learns through direct contact—by trying, failing, and trying again. It's ridiculously character-building. And yes, it builds self-esteem... but the tuition is steep.

Sometimes I don't even realize what I've learned until I've sat through the **emotional hangover**—after the sadness, disappointment, anxiety, or frustration has had its say. There are moments I feel completely defeated. Sometimes I literally have to do things twice: reading a sentence, writing an email, finishing a book.

It can feel like I'm broken. Like, why can't I get it the first time? I've even wondered if I have undiagnosed ADHD. (And for the record, a DNA test confirmed I carry a gene expression linked to distractibility—but that's not the same as classic ADD. That's a rabbit hole for Book Two. Or maybe a podcast.)

There are days I have to slam the laptop shut, walk out of my apartment, and head straight to the beach to reset. I've jumped into the ocean fully clothed, letting the salt water strip off the emotional gunk of another failed attempt. Other times, I've biked to South Pointe in yoga clothes, no plan, no bra, no f*cks given—just needing to escape the sludge of another hard-earned lesson.

In those moments, I've yelled—at the sky, at Mother Nature, maybe even at God:

- Why do I have to learn everything the hard way?
- Why does it feel like life is uphill while other people just coast?
- Why am I always the one tripping and falling face-first into the next spiritual "lesson"?

And seriously—if one more spiritual person tells me "they're not mistakes, they're learning experiences," I'm going to lose it. After a sh*t ton of mistakes, guess what? I'm starting to get pretty f*cking smart. (Bitterness fully intended.)

The Bitterness Crucible

Being a 3/5 Projector with Ego Authority and seven open centers isn't just intense—it's a **soul crucible**. It creates a kind of energetic pressure that forces presence. A stranglehold on your system that says: Let go. You figured out another way that doesn't work. Feel it. Integrate it. Start again.

To survive, I've thrown everything at it—therapy, life coaching, Human Design readings, energy work, crystal bathing at the Integratron, pranayama breathwork, digital detox camps, screaming into the ocean... you name it. Not because I'm obsessed with healing, but because I need tools to get through the day. There is so much conditioning to get rid of, be aware of and let go of. (This mashup of Projector, seven open centers, right mind, 3/5 profile, and the rarest authority... ugh.)

Sometimes, these tools work. When I pause, reflect, cry, swim, scream, journal, vent, or call my therapist, I catch glimpses of the bigger picture. I start to **see the lesson**, the growth, the wisdom I didn't even know was forming.

It's subtle. It's not like I wake up one day feeling like a guru. But over time, something shifts. When I'm faced with a new situation, question, or challenge—I respond in ways that surprise even me. Suddenly, I'm saying things I didn't even know I knew. I'm answering questions with clarity. I'm watching myself speak and thinking:

Wow... who is this wise boss bitch? Did that just come out of me? Damn, I'm brilliant.

It's like the wisdom was **downloaded straight from the chaos**. Not from a class. Not from a book. But from living it.

That's the gift (ugh, fine... the gift) of the 3/5. You become an expert not because someone taught you—but because you survived the fire and came out with something worth saying.

Am I grateful? Eventually.

Do I still struggle to accept this is how I work? Absolutely.

Do I love it? Not exactly.

YAY. (Sarcasm completely intended.)

Enter the 5: The Heretic, The Problem-Solver

And that's just the 3-line in me—the experimenter, the one who learns by living, failing, and trying again. The 5 adds an entirely different flavor: the heretic, the rescuer, the problem-solver. The one onto whom people can't help but project their hopes, expectations, and sometimes their salvation fantasies.

When you combine them, you get a life that's equal parts laboratory and classroom. Everything becomes a test, a teaching moment, or both.

In my more irreverent explanations of the 5th line, I like to joke that Jesus must have been a 5th line. People projected their unmet needs onto him, begged for miracles, and when their expectations weren't met—well, they nailed him to a cross. Having the 5 in your profile is a bit like living that parable in modern form: people will see what they need to see in you, not necessarily who you are.

The 5th line is the Projection Field—a mirror for others' desires. People feel your potential to solve their problems, to lead, to fix. Sometimes you can. Sometimes that projection is simply their own reflection asking to be seen. The real mastery is learning what's yours to carry and what's not.

So yes, the 3/5 Projector life is messy, brilliant, exhausting, and enlightening—all at once. It's the sacred mayhem of trial, error, revelation, and reform. And somehow, against all logic, it feels exactly right.

21

Embracing the Projector Experiment

In the Human Design system, one phrase comes up again and again:

Follow your Strategy and Authority.

For Projectors, that means *waiting to be invited*—and then using your *Inner Authority* to determine whether the invitation is correct for you.

But here's the thing: to receive an invitation, people need to know who the hell you are.

You have to be **visible**. You have to be **recognized**.

The world can't invite you if you're invisible to it.

That's why so many Human Design books and teachers say:

Projectors should learn something deeply.

Become an expert. Be known for something. Study, study, study what you enjoy.

Once you're recognized for your gifts, it naturally creates more opportunities to be invited.

It's a feedback loop:

Recognition builds reputation, and reputation attracts aligned invitations.

And that's when the real experiment begins—*following your Strategy and Authority* to make decisions from a place of authenticity rather than conditioning.

The Shift: Stop Forcing, Start Waiting

When I first sat with this information, something shifted.

I realized I had been inviting myself to the party my entire life—forcing my way into situations, initiating opportunities, and trying to prove my value without waiting for the right timing.

I decided to give the Projector experiment a real shot.

Like a dedicated researcher, I began to observe my life through this new lens. I asked myself constantly:

- Am I being recognized?
- Am I being seen clearly?
- Is this an actual invitation—and is it one I even want to accept?
- Is this situation I'm currently in, come to me via an invitation?

Over the years, I've refined the process. Now I ask myself:

Does this feel like a yummy invitation?

If the answer is yes, I check in with my **Ego Center** (also called the Will Center) to see if I have the energy, willpower, and stamina to follow through.

For me, that's my Inner Authority—and it never steers me wrong when I really listen.

Taking Aligned Action

When all the pieces align—

Recognition,

Invitation,

That yummy internal "yes,"

and the energetic capacity to follow through—

that's when I move.

Not before.

That shift has transformed how I approach everything—from work to relationships to creativity.

Instead of pushing, proving, or hustling, I **wait**.

I **listen**.

I **check in**.

And when I move, I move with **clarity and conviction**.

Viewing It as an Experiment

Viewing this as an *experiment* has been key.

It protects me from spiraling into self-pity or bitterness when things aren't flowing.

Because when you frame it as a personal experiment, you're no longer failing—

You're collecting data.

You're learning what works and what doesn't.

That mindset turns every disappointment into useful information. It's necessary to reframe it or you'll die of bitterness.

The Point of It All

And that, ultimately, is the point of the Human Design experiment:

To **decondition** from everything the world has projected onto you (no pun intended),

and to discover the unique, differentiated version of yourself that you were actually born to be.

So whether it's invitations, visibility, or resting when I'm not recognized, I remind myself:

This is all part of the process.

I'm not here to be everything to everyone.

I'm here to be unmistakably me—

and to wait for the people who see that to extend the right invitations.

22

Why My Profile Makes Me a Natural Biohacker

Being a **3/5** means I'm wired for self-experimentation — which is basically the definition of biohacking. I don't just read about something; I test it.

Take red light therapy. People rave about its benefits, but when I tried it, I didn't notice much. Maybe it's all marketing hype, or maybe I'm not "sick enough" to see the difference — either way, I needed to experience it myself to know.

Or the time I tried being vegan. Supposedly "the best" diet. For me? My cholesterol went up, and so did my hemoglobin A1c. Lesson learned: no more lettuce-only living.

Then there was the advice from a well-known male bio-hacker about eating 30 grams of protein within 30 minutes of waking. I followed it — and promptly gained weight. Thanks for sharing, GB.

Here's the thing: in a **3-line life, "failure" isn't failure.** It's data. Every dead end is one more variable eliminated. Every detour sharpens the map. Every experiment — whether it "works" or not — becomes another layer of wisdom I can share, both in my own life and with my client

Why My Clients Benefit From My 3/5 Profile

Because I've already face-planted through a lot of the trial-and-error phase, I can spot red flags faster for the people I work with. If you tell me you're thinking of buying a $4,000 ozone sauna, I can walk you through the pros, cons, and "oh, by the way, here's what no one tells you about the installation process."

The "5" in me can hand you a shortcut — a tried-and-tested solution — but the "3" will always keep me grounded in the reality that *your* experience will still need to be personalized. I can hand you my results, but you still have to run your own experiment.

For my clients who also have a 3/5 profile, I always wish I could magically take away your pain, but I can't. I can support you to the best of my ability so you too can gain the wisdom I am finally beginning to acquire. Come my warrior children, let's go!

Breaking the "No Self-Disclosure" Rule

Coming from a background in psychology, I was initially trained not to self-disclose. Therapists are taught to stay neutral and not share too much of their personal lives. But that approach never quite fit how my 3/5 nature learns or connects.

One of the biggest reasons I love being a psychological life coach is that I'm not bound by those old-school therapeutic constraints. It gives me the freedom to work intuitively and use methods that are both efficient and customized to the unique human in front of me.

Sometimes, self-disclosure isn't a boundary violation — it's a bridge. Clients often trust counselors, coaches, and mentors who've walked through similar darkness and come out the other side. Knowing I've been there gives them permission to believe healing is possible. The 3/5 path is about turning your lived experiments into maps that others can follow, if they choose.

Biohacking + 3/5 Mindset in Action

When I reversed my biological age by 15 months in just 3 months, it didn't happen because I followed a perfect protocol from a book. It happened because I:

1. Took an honest look at what *wasn't* working (even the stuff I thought was "healthy").
2. Was willing to throw things out and start fresh.
3. Stopped following generalized advice and doubled down on what was correct for my chart — my digestion type, my environment, and my Ego Authority.

That's the beauty of a 3/5 life: the setbacks feed the breakthroughs. And when you embrace that, you stop fearing "failure" and start seeing it as an essential part of the process.

Profiles tell you how you learn and live—but Human Design also shows you where you're most open, conditioned, and vulnerable to distraction. Up next, we'll explore the Open Centers and the shadow themes that shape (and often distort) our lives.

IV

Open Centers & 7 Years of Deconditioning

23

Deconditioning, Depth, and Discovering Who I'm Not

Human Design—alongside many other personal development tools I've explored over the years—has profoundly transformed my life. But unlike some modalities that offer quick fixes or temporary clarity, Human Design is a system of deep, ongoing experimentation. It's a living laboratory, and I've been running experiments in mine for over eight years.

My very first Human Design reading was in December 2016. Fast forward to September 2025, and I've had 19 different Human Design professional exposures—through certified analyst readings, immersive classes at the BG5 Institute and the International School of Human Design, and global gatherings like the international HD festival in Bulgaria and the High Desert Human Design conference. With each encounter, I added a new layer to my understanding. But more than that, I tested everything in real time. I paid attention to what happened when I followed my Strategy and Authority. I watched how my energy responded, how my relationships shifted, and how life opened—or closed—based on whether I was living in alignment.

Over time, one thing became crystal clear: When I live in alignment with my design, life flows. I find myself in the right place, at the right time, with the right people. I'm invited, recognized, and successful—not just professionally, but energetically.

Let me legitimize myself for a moment: I didn't just discover Human Design a couple of years ago and decide to write a book. I've been in it—living it, studying it, questioning it, and sometimes resisting it—for nearly a decade. At one point, I even had a T-shirt made with my bodygraph printed on the back. That way, at the HD festival in Bulgaria, other attendees could tell at a glance that I was a Projector and knew to invite me into conversation. (Yes, that's immersion. And yes, that's very Human Design nerd behavior.)

That festival ended up being a real turning point. People kept approaching me with a mix of curiosity and fascination. They'd glance at my chart and ask:

"What's it like to have seven open centers?"

"What's it like to have only one defined channel?"

"What's it like to be born on the Cross of Penetration?"

They were particularly intrigued by my Channel of Shock, my defined Heart, and the penetrating aura of a Projector. My honest answer? I don't know anything different. This is simply how I've always been. But what I do know is this: I've come to embrace my design not just as a system, but as a guide for making sense of life. It's helped me make better decisions, form more aligned relationships, and experience a younger, more vibrant version of myself—inside and out.

While in Bulgaria, one question kept coming up:

"When were you first introduced to Human Design?"

When I finally did the math, I realized something that stopped me in my tracks: I had officially crossed the seven-year mark.

If you're familiar with Human Design, you've probably heard about the seven-year deconditioning cycle. This is the idea that when you begin living in alignment with your Type, Strategy, and Authority, your body and mind start to release the conditioning you've absorbed throughout your life. Cellular memory begins to shift. Neurological patterns can start to rewire. But the process doesn't start until you're aware of your design—and committed to living it.

For me, that deconditioning wasn't a linear journey. It was curvy. A loop of experimenting, resisting, learning, integrating, messing up, feeling bitterness, and recalibrating.

Standing in Bulgaria, surrounded by fellow Human Design explorers, I had a moment of stillness. I looked around and realized: I had completed something. Not in a "mission accomplished" kind of way—but in a cellular, embodied way. I could feel the lightness in my system. A quiet certainty. A groundedness I had never quite accessed before.

Later that day, I met another Projector—a woman who splits her time between Berlin and Ibiza. She works with people on shadow integration and openness, and when we connected, she didn't exactly encourage me—she challenged me. She honed in on something in my field, noting a clarity and vibrancy that suggested I had recently moved through something significant. Her words landed sharply but mean-ingfully. She acknowledged the strength of my Ego Authority and reminded me—pointedly—that I can have what I want, if I own it. She also pushed me to consider how I might support others in working with their own shadows, especially given the radical openness in my chart. (7 open centers, 2 defined centers) And she was right.

What's shifted the most since then is my relationship to the open parts of my chart. For years, I was fixated on what was defined—what I had. But now, I'm far more curious about what I don't have. What's open. Where I'm most vulnerable to conditioning, yes—but also where I'm most capable of deep, embodied wisdom.

During our conversation, she said something that struck a deep chord:

"With all your openness and shadow themes, you need to check in with your nervous system multiple times a day. Grounding yourself isn't optional—it's essential."

Her words hit hard. I hadn't fully considered the toll that constant openness can take. That night, I returned to my hotel room and took an entire day for myself. Coincidentally—or maybe perfectly timed—I had come down with a cold, so I stayed in bed. But instead of feeling frustrated, I treated it as an opportunity for integration. I was upstairs in the conference hotel, watching snow fall softly over the rooftops of Sofia, Bulgaria, while letting my body and aura recalibrate.

Luckily, the sessions were being streamed on Zoom, so I didn't miss anything. But more importantly, I realized something profound: To truly complete this first seven-year cycle of deconditioning, I needed to become more attuned to how my openness makes me vulnerable to outside energy—and more intentional about how I restore and protect my system.

After the festival, I spent a bonus day alone in London before flying back to the U.S. I walked the city, deeply contemplated things, found my 'internal markets' coworking space to think clearly. I needed that space to process everything that had just moved through me. That day felt different. Eerie, even. I wouldn't call it a spiritual experience—because I've never really identified with that language—but it was damn close. There were so many synchronicities that I stopped keeping track. But it wasn't just the coincidences. It was the state I was in: completely connected to my system, like something had clicked into place.

It didn't feel like a mental high. It wasn't coming from my open mind (undefined head center) or from someone else's aura. It wasn't conditioned by someone else's defined centers or vibes. I was literally staying in a hotel room below ground level—in the basement—tucked into the belly of the Earth. Maybe it was some powerful neutrinos having their way with me, who knows. But what I *can* say is this: something shifted. A tipping point was crossed. My awareness felt blasted open.

Maybe it's what people mean when they talk about their third eye opening. Whatever it was, I'm not interested in over-analyzing it. I'm just deeply grateful it happened—and that I had the presence to notice.

Sometimes, the real transformation doesn't happen in the workshop. It happens in the quiet. In the rest. In the solitude.

And this was one of those moments.

Seven-Year Deconditioning

Deconditioning is the process of releasing patterns that aren't truly you.
It takes about seven years for cellular renewal, but the process begins the moment you live by Type,

Strategy, and Authority.
It isn't linear--it's experimental, messy, and
deeply human.
The result isn't "perfection"--it's awareness,
clarity, and more consistent alignment.

*Deconditioning revealed another truth: where you're open,
you're vulnerable. My chart has seven open centers, and each
comes with a shadow theme—patterns that can hijack your
energy if you don't see them coming. Understanding those
shadows changed how I coach, how I biohack, and how I live.
Let's go look at your definition first.*

24

Defined Centers

In Human Design, whether a center is defined (colored in) or open (white) in your chart is determined by the precise positions of celestial bodies—the sun, moon, planets, and the lunar nodes—at the moment of your birth and approximately 88 days prior. These two moments together imprint your conscious and unconscious design influences.

Each planet's placement activates specific gates—energetic doorways linked to the 64 I Ching hexagrams—within the nine centers. When two gates at either end of a channel are both activated by these planetary positions, the channel connecting two centers becomes defined. As a result, those centers become defined as well, representing consistent, reliable sources of energy that manifest as durable traits, behaviors, or ways of processing energy.

Defined centers indicate energy that is fixed and reliable in your life. They generate and process energy consistently, creating what you can think of as your unique internal "energetic architecture." These centers form your energetic constants—the parts of your design that tend to feel most "you" and stable over time.

In contrast, open or undefined centers, shown as white areas on your chart, are more fluid and receptive. They do not produce consistent energy but instead absorb and amplify the energies of others and the environment. This openness provides adaptability and heightened perception but also vulnerability to conditioning, which can mask your authentic self.

The Blueprint Analogy

Imagine an architect's blueprint—the foundational structure of a building. Once the framework is set, it remains mostly fixed, shaping the building's form and function. Similarly, your Human Design chart is fixed at birth based on planetary geometry, with black lines representing conscious traits and red lines reflecting unconscious aspects.

Together, your defined and open centers create this blueprint for your energetic design: defined centers as the solid framework, open centers as flexible spaces adapting to surroundings.

The Nine Centers and Their Major Themes

Each center governs specific life themes, both physical and psychological. When defined, they provide stable access to those energies:

- Head (Inspiration): Mental pressure to question, imagine, and inspire. Defined Heads offer consistent insight and thought stimulation.
- Ajna (Conceptualization): The processing center for ideas and beliefs. Defined Ajnas hold fixed mental impressions and analytical stability.
- Throat (Communication & Manifestation): Expression

and transformation. Defined Throats reliably channel energy into speech, creativity, and action.

- G Center (Identity & Direction): The core of purpose and love. Defined G Centers have a steady sense of self and life direction.
- Heart/Ego (Willpower & Value): Governs motivation, self-worth, and material drive. Defined Hearts continuously provide willpower.
- Solar Plexus (Emotional Awareness): The emotional wave. Defined Solar Plexus centers experience consistent emotional rhythms.
- Sacral (Life Force & Work): Source of sustained energy. Defined Sacrals generate dependable vitality and response energy.
- Spleen (Instinct & Intuition): Center of health and survival instincts. Defined Spleens offer steady intuitive and immune senses.
- Root (Stress & Drive): Pressure center for action and evolution. Defined Roots channel stress into productive energy consistently.

Awareness and Deconditioning

In Human Design, deconditioning—the process of shedding external influences to reconnect with your authentic design—typically takes about seven years. This involves releasing expectation-driven behaviors, learning to trust your unique authority, and coming home to yourself energetically and psychologically. Understanding your defined and open centers is foundational to this process, as it helps clarify which energies are inherently yours and which belong to the conditioning of your environment.In Human Design, whether a center is defined (colored in) or open (white) in your chart is determined by the precise positions of celestial bodies—the sun, moon, planets, and the lunar nodes—at the moment of your birth and approximately 88 days prior. These two moments together imprint your conscious and unconscious design influences.

Each planet's placement activates specific gates—energetic doorways linked to the 64 I Ching hexagrams—within the nine centers. When two gates at either end of a channel are both activated by these planetary positions, the channel connecting two centers becomes defined. As a result, those centers become defined as well, representing consistent, reliable sources of energy that manifest as durable traits, behaviors, or ways of processing energy.

Defined centers indicate energy that is fixed and reliable in your life. They generate and process energy consistently, creating what you can think of as your unique internal "energetic architecture." These centers form your energetic constants—the parts of your design that tend to feel most "you" and stable over time.

In contrast, open or undefined centers, shown as white areas on your chart, are more fluid and receptive. They do not produce consistent energy but instead absorb and amplify the energies of others and the environment. This openness provides adaptability and heightened perception but also vulnerability to conditioning, which can mask your authentic self.

The Blueprint Analogy

Imagine an architect's blueprint—the foundational structure of a building. Once the framework is set, it remains mostly fixed, shaping the building's form and function. Similarly, your Human Design chart is fixed at birth based on planetary geometry, with black lines representing conscious traits and red lines reflecting unconscious aspects.

Together, your defined and open centers create this blueprint for your energetic design: defined centers as the solid framework, open centers as flexible spaces adapting to surroundings.

The Nine Centers and Their Major Themes

Each center governs specific life themes, both physical and psychological. When defined, they provide stable access to those energies:

- **Head** (Inspiration): Mental pressure to question, imagine, and inspire. Defined Heads offer consistent insight and thought stimulation.
- **Ajna** (Conceptualization): The processing center for ideas and beliefs. Defined Ajnas hold fixed mental impressions and analytical stability.
- **Throat** (Communication & Manifestation): Expression and transformation. Defined Throats reliably channel energy into speech, creativity, and action.
- **G Center** (Identity & Direction): The core of purpose and love. Defined G Centers have a steady sense of self and life direction.
- **Heart/Ego** (Willpower & Value): Governs motivation, self-worth, and material drive. Defined Hearts continuously provide willpower.
- **Solar Plexus** (Emotional Awareness): The emotional wave. Defined Solar Plexus centers experience consistent emotional rhythms.

- **Sacral** (Life Force & Work): Source of sustained energy. Defined Sacrals generate dependable vitality and response energy.
- **Spleen** (Instinct & Intuition): Center of health and survival instincts. Defined Spleens offer steady intuitive and immune senses.
- **Root** (Stress & Drive): Pressure center for action and evolution. Defined Roots channel stress into productive energy consistently.

Awareness and Deconditioning

In Human Design, deconditioning—the process of shedding external influences to reconnect with your authentic design—typically takes about seven years. This involves releasing expectation-driven behaviors, learning to trust your unique authority, and coming home to yourself energetically and psychologically. Understanding your defined and open centers is foundational to this process, as it helps clarify which energies are inherently yours and which belong to the conditioning of your environment.

25

Undefined Centers: Shadows, Distractions & Wisdom

Earlier, I shared the moment I began to understand my own openness — the places in my chart where I'm most vulnerable to outside influence. In Human Design, these are called Undefined or Open Centers. They're like energetic sponges: they soak up, amplify, and sometimes distort the energy of the people and environments around us.

This is where the shadow themes live. It's where we're most likely to get distracted, conditioned, or pulled off our path — and also where the biggest potential for wisdom lies. Over time, as you start noticing the patterns, these open areas become your deepest teachers.

The key is to recognize when you're acting from conditioning rather than your truth. Once you see it, you can step back, reset, and choose differently. Each open center carries a "tell" — a signature shadow question — that lets you know you're slipping into distraction or the not-self. Spotting these tells has been one of the most radical shifts Human Design has given me, and I see the same thing happen for my clients once they start paying attention.

The Nine Centers & Their Shadow Questions

Below are the nine centers, the "shadow questions" that signal conditioning, and how to start reframing them into sources of wisdom.

Head (Inspiration)

Shadow Question: Am I thinking about things that don't matter?

Distraction: Scattering energy on thoughts that don't matter.

No gates: You may not even know what's interesting to you.

Wisdom Potential: Clarity about which questions are truly worth pursuing.

Biohacking Tip: Limit input streams (social media, constant news) so your mind has space to recover. Mental rest is as important as sleep.

Ajna (Conceptualization)

Shadow Question: Am I trying to convince everyone I'm certain?

Distraction: Defending shaky opinions, pretending to be sure.

No gates: You may not know what to think or what's worth being certain about.

Wisdom Potential: Flexibility and openness to multiple perspectives.

Biohacking Tip: Practice pausing before forming conclusions. This lowers stress chemistry tied to "needing to be right."

Throat (Communication)

   Shadow Question: Am I trying to attract attention?

   Distraction: Speaking just to be heard, oversharing.

   No gates: You may not know what to say or when to say it.

   Wisdom Potential: Learning timing — when your words carry the most impact.

   Biohacking Tip: Track how you feel after speaking. Speech aligned with timing sustains energy instead of draining it.

G / Self (Identity)

Shadow Question: Am I looking for direction and love?

Distraction: Shape-shifting to fit in or chasing identity through others.

No gates: You may not know what to be.

Wisdom Potential: Sensitivity to place and belonging. You know when a space or role feels right.

Biohacking Tip: Prioritize environments where you feel at home. This is as biologically important as diet or exercise.

Ego / Heart (Willpower)

Shadow Question: Am I trying to prove myself?

Distraction: Overcommitting, overworking, overcompensating.

No gates: You may not know what's worth proving.

Wisdom Potential: Recognizing true value — when energy and will are worth it.

Biohacking Tip: Pause before saying yes. If the desire isn't there, conserving energy protects your vitality.

Spleen (Intuition)

Shadow Question: Am I holding on to what isn't good for me?

Distraction: Clinging to habits, relationships, or environments out of fear.

No gates: You may not know what to fear or what intuition feels like.

Wisdom Potential: Over time, you become wise about what's healthy and safe.

Biohacking Tip: Do weekly "body scans." Notice which habits feel nourishing and which feel draining — then release accordingly.

Sacral (Life Force)

Shadow Question: Do I know when enough is enough?

Distraction: Overdoing, burning out, trying to keep up.

No gates: You may not know where to apply energy.

Wisdom Potential: Teaching others discernment about sustainable energy use.

Biohacking Tip: Schedule rest. For non-Sacrals, downtime is not optional; it keeps cortisol from driving premature aging.

Solar Plexus (Emotions)

Shadow Question: Am I avoiding confrontation and truth?

Distraction: Avoiding conflict, amplifying others' moods.

No gates: You may not know what to feel.

Wisdom Potential: Deep clarity about emotional dynamics when you learn to separate yours from others.

Biohacking Tip: Breathwork or journaling helps release amplified emotions that aren't yours.

Root (Pressure)

    Shadow Question: Am I in a hurry just to escape pressure?

Distraction: Chronic rushing, urgency addiction.

No gates: You may not know when pressure is necessary.

Wisdom Potential: Sensitivity to real versus false pressure. You can teach others how to pace themselves.

    Biohacking Tip: Experiment with "pressure fasts." Take intentional pauses where you do nothing and watch how your system responds.

```
Quick Guide to the Nine Centers & Their Shadow
Questions
Head (Inspiration): Am I thinking about things that
```

don't matter?
Ajna (Conceptualization): Am I trying to convince
everyone I'm certain?
Throat (Communication): Am I trying to attract
attention?
G/Self (Identity): Am I looking for direction and
love?
Ego/Heart (Willpower): Am I trying to prove myself?
Splenic (Intuition): Am I holding on to what isn't
good for me?
Sacral (Life Force): Do I know when enough is enough?
Solar Plexus (Emotions): Am I avoiding confrontation
and truth?
Root (Pressure): Am I rushing just to escape
pressure?

How This Looks in Real Life

Open Head & Ajna: After coffee with someone whose Head was defined, I left buzzing with ideas—none of which mattered to my actual goals. By the end of the day, I realized I'd wasted hours researching *their* ideas and ended up bitter because I could have used that time and energy on my own path. This actually happened with 2 different potential podcast partners.

Open Solar Plexus: For years, I avoided confrontation at all costs. I'd smooth things over just to keep the peace—even when I wasn't wrong. Now, I pause, breathe, and check: *Is this even my emotion?* Then I communicate gently and effectively. Most of the time, I can spin the truth in a way that ends up being win/win. Slowly I have learned that confrontation and truth aren't that scary.

Open Throat: Sometimes I catch myself trying to post too much on social media—or using sexuality or my body to attract likes. When I notice this, I immediately stop and delete whatever I was curating because I can see my shadow trying to be seen. Anytime I catch myself, "trying" instead of just "being" it's usually this open throat being conditioned by some outside force.

Open Spleen: When I start reconsidering getting back together with an ex—or doing business with someone selfish or lazy—I stop and check myself. (I share a very funny story about this later in the dating section.) Earlier today I received a call asking me to come back to an old collaboration gig, but luckily I've learned to stop holding on to what isn't good for me. No thank you, I respectfully declined.

Open Sacral Center: Working too much. Eating too much. Dancing too much. You get the point. I've learned when enough is enough.

Open Root Center: When I show up early to an event and get bitter because the host isn't starting on time. When a sliding-scale client wants more time than we agreed to and I feel resentful. When I get trapped in a conversation too long, "being nice," even though I'm exhausted and bored. The pressure of the Root can keep me there way longer than I want to.

Open Ego: Mine is defined, so I don't have a ton of life experience here — but I do know what it looks like when I've acted from the "not-self" of the open Ego. Once, I signed up for a half marathon simply to prove I could. That single question — *Do I actually want this, or am I just trying to prove myself?* — is everything.

Open G: Mine is defined as well, but before deconditioning, I can spot where I was operating from the "not-self" here too. Signing up for dating apps again out of restlessness. Browsing job listings and fantasizing about using my degrees to do something else entirely. Entertaining the idea of working for someone else instead of continuing as a solo-preneur.

26

Real-Time Awareness: From Dance Floors to Dinner Plates

Once I really grasped how my openness worked, I started running little experiments — sometimes on purpose, sometimes by accident.

One of my favorite "accidental" experiments happened on a night out dancing. The DJ was on fire, the crowd was electric, and I felt like I could stay on the dance floor until sunrise. It wasn't until I stepped outside for air that I realized — nope. I was done. My legs were jelly, my energy tank was empty, and I was suddenly fantasizing about my bed. That's when it hit me: I'd been surfing on everyone else's Sacral energy all night. The second I stepped out of the Generators' auras, the wave crashed.

Now, I know that if I'm going to ride that kind of energy, I have to plan for the drop. Same goes for the gym. If I'm lifting weights next to a Generator, my reps are cleaner, my rest times are shorter, and I feel like a champ. But the moment they leave? I'm ready for a nap and a protein shake.

This kind of real-time awareness has completely changed the way I approach biohacking:

- **In the gym**: I focus on quality over quantity, and I'm strategic about who I stand next to.
- **At social events**: I pace myself, knowing that borrowed energy is just that — borrowed.
- **In my kitchen**: I eat according to my digestion type, even if that means politely dodging a brunch invite. I catch myself over eating when I eat with Generators, when I'm not aware.

The beautiful thing is, when you combine your Human Design awareness with biohacking, you stop trying to be everything all the time. You start making micro-adjustments that keep you in your own lane — which is the only lane where your energy flows effortlessly.

And here's the part I didn't expect: It made me more compassionate toward other people. When I could see their energy patterns clearly, I stopped taking their moods, habits, or even their projections personally. Most of the time, it wasn't about me. And when it *was* about me, I was clear enough to respond with choice instead of reaction.

Once I understood my open centers and stopped letting them run the show, life started to feel calmer and clearer. But there was still one huge piece of the puzzle missing — how I was actually nourishing myself.

Enter Variables — the four arrows at the top of your Human Design chart. These are like your body's settings for how you best take in food, information, and the world around you. The first arrow we'll explore is Digestion (also called Determination), which holds the secret to when, where, and how your body thrives on nourishment — and, as I discovered, how it can even help you reverse aging.

V

Variables (The Arrows)

27

Variables: The Deeper Keys in Your Chart

At the very top of your Human Design chart, you'll see four little arrows—two red, two black—pointing either left or right. These are called **Variables**, and they represent some of the most advanced (and practical) layers of the system.

Each arrow points to a key area of how your system is designed to operate:

- **Top Left (red): Determination** → how you digest food, information, and life itself.
- **Bottom Left (red): Environment** → the physical and energetic spaces where your body thrives.
- **Top Right (black): Perspective** → how you're meant to see the world.
- **Bottom Right (black): Motivation** → what truly drives you at a deep level.

For this book, I'm focusing on the first two—**Digestion (Determination)** and **Environment**—because they were the biggest needle-movers in my biohacking journey. These weren't just "fun facts" from a chart. They were game-changers. They tipped the needle on my labs, my body composition, my sleep, and most impressively, my biological age.

Most biohackers focus on external tools—cold plunges, red light therapy, fasting windows, supplement stacks. All of that can help. But if you're running those protocols *against your design*, you're grinding gears. Human Design gives you the missing context—the internal operating system that shows you how your biology actually wants to function.

That's why I'm starting here. Because while Strategy and Inner Authority give you the foundation for decision-making, **Variables fine-tune your biology day-to-day.**

28

Digestion: My Vampire Hack That Changed Everything

In Human Design, **Digestion Type** (also called **Determination**) is part of the **Primary Health System (PHS)**. It's not about *what* you eat — it's about *how* your system is designed to take in nourishment and information.

Think of it as the conditions your body needs in order to actually absorb and use what you put in. Some people need consistency, others need variety. Some thrive in quiet spaces, others in active environments. It's not about restriction or following the latest food trend — it's about aligning with your unique design.

Why This Matters for Biohacking

Your Digestion Type is like a personalized operating manual for your metabolism, your brain, and even your nervous system.

- **It's not about calories.** It's about conditions.
- **It's not about rules.** It's about awareness.
- **It's not about self-denial.** It's about discovering when and how your body thrives.

Once you understand this, you can drop the endless cycle of generic diet advice and finally start listening to what your system actually wants.

```
Biohacking Tip
Your Digestion Type isn't about restriction. It's
about conditions.
Pay attention to when and how your body wants to eat.
Forget "one-size-fits-all" diets. Aligning with your
```

design brings better results -- and more joy.

Get Your Birth Time Right

Here's the thing: accuracy matters. Digestion (and the other Variables like Environment) are calculated from the fine details of your birth chart. That means your birth time needs to be as accurate as possible.

I know we all want to believe our moms remember the exact minute we were born — but please verify. Most birth certificates or official records list the time, and if not, hospitals and county courthouses often keep archives.

Personally, I use the **Maia Mechanics software**, which even provides a reliability score if you only have an estimated time. For example, just yesterday, I had a coaching client from Egypt who only knew she was born sometime between 2–5 p.m. The software showed the only chart shift happened 40 minutes before 2 p.m.—so we could confidently proceed with her reading.

If no records exist, there are "reverse astrologers" who can help you reconstruct a chart based on life events. As a last resort, you can run your own experiment and rely on Strategy and Authority to feel out what works best for your body. Treat it like a biohacking trial — your biology will always reveal what's true. I know the software costs money so if you want to book an appointment with me I can look up your "reliability score" as part of our session together.

Big Picture

Digestion Types describe **how you're built to take things in** — food, information, and experiences. Each type also has an Active (Left) or Passive (Right) orientation, which fine-tunes how your system operates.

This isn't about dieting. It's not a fad. It's your constitutional design. And when you live in sync with it, your body responds: better energy, better labs, better aging.

Here are the **12 Digestion Types**:

1. **Consecutive Appetite (Left/Active)** – Eat one simple food at a time, no mixing. Simplicity is key.
2. **Alternating Appetite (Right/Passive)** – Flexible one-

food-at-a-time eating. Flow and rotation work best.

3. **Open Taste (Left/Active)** – Thrives on variety and experimentation. Nourished by new flavors.

4. **Closed Taste (Right/Passive)** – Prefers consistency. Familiar foods are easiest to digest.

5. **Hot Thirst (Left/Active)** – Best with warm or hot food/drink. Cold can feel jarring. Above your body temperature.

6. **Cold Thirst (Right/Passive)** – Favors cool or room-temp food and drinks. Below you body temperature.

7. **Calm Touch (Left/Active)** – Needs quiet, still spaces to digest properly.

8. **Nervous Touch (Right/Passive)** – Digestion is activated by movement, talking, stimulation.

9. **High Sound (Left/Active)** – Stimulated by lively soundscapes (music, conversation, city noise).

10. **Low Sound (Right/Passive)** – Thrives in quiet or gentle soundscapes.

11. **Direct Light (Left/Active)** – Best digestion in daylight, especially bright sunlight.

12. **Indirect Light (Right/Passive)** – Best digestion in dim or indirect light—at night, indoors, or in shadowed places.

My Indirect Light Digestion Experiment

Of all the biohacks I've tried, this has been the single most transformative.

In Human Design, Digestion isn't just about food. It's about how your body takes in *everything* — nourishment, information, even experiences. For me, my Digestion Type is **Indirect Light (Right)**, which means I thrive when I eat in dim or shadowed spaces, away from direct sunlight — at night, or in low-light environments.

At first, I thought: *Seriously? Eat in the dark like a vampire?* But when I tested it — everything changed.

- At sunny picnics, I'd lose my appetite completely.
- Forcing down "healthy" breakfasts left me bloated and sluggish.
- Eating late at night — something mainstream advice warns against — actually helped me sleep better and wake up lighter.
- Midnight snacks, far from being a guilty habit, became a key to better rest.

Once I stopped fighting my rhythm and started living it, my body responded almost immediately. My labs improved. My body fat dropped. Food finally felt like an ally instead of a stressor. I only ate when I was actually hungry.

Enter: My Inner Vampire

This experiment became so much a part of me that I started calling myself a **happy vampire biohacker**. My friends all joke, "Julie drinks the blood at night," and honestly, it's become a kind of tagline. Blackout curtains, shadow dinners, and midnight snacks have turned into my longevity toolkit.

When I first learned about this, my Human Design advisor laughed and said:

"Welcome to being a vampire. You drink blood at night, and the sunlight burns your skin."

We cracked up, but it stuck — because it was the first biohack that wasn't trendy, generic, or one-size-fits-all. It was designed for me.

How I Applied It (and Why It Worked)

Once I started eating in alignment with Indirect Light, I fell into a rhythm that matched my biology:

- A light lunch with vitamins, nothing heavy
- Afternoon naps behind blackout curtains, waking refreshed
- Two dinners — one early, one later at night
- Midnight snacks that actually improved my sleep

This flew in the face of conventional biohacking advice. For example, when I forced myself to follow the famous "30 grams of protein within 30 minutes of waking" rule, I actually gained weight. When I pushed myself into early breakfasts because "that's what healthy people do," my digestion rebelled.

But when I honored my design, my blood work improved, my energy stabilized, and for the first time in years, eating felt joyful again.

Sometimes that looked unconventional: fasting most of the day, sipping coffee, matcha lattes with collagen powder, a powerbar and saving my "real" eating for after dark. My doctor even confirmed the results:

- Lower A1c
- Better cholesterol
- Less body fat

All while enjoying carrot cake whenever I wanted. I have to eat my vegetables somehow. Don't worry I keep it in moderation.

Practical Vampire Hack

If you're Indirect Light like me:

- Don't force daytime meals.
- Blackout curtains are your best friend.
- Night eating doesn't mean overeating — it means eating when your body is ready to process. For many, that looks like saving the bulk of calories for after sunset.
- Try socializing over cozy late dinners instead of sunny brunches.
- If you don't eat during the day it doesn't mean you have an eating disorder

The Lesson

The biggest anti-aging secret isn't always a supplement, gadget, or protocol. Sometimes it's hidden in your design.

When you feed your body in the way it's built to thrive, you get to ditch the "shoulds," stop fighting with food, and reclaim the joy of eating. And joy itself — the ease of being aligned with who you are — is one of the most powerful anti-aging hacks there is.

If Digestion shows you how your body takes in nourishment,
Environment *shows you where your body belongs. When I paired my Indirect Light digestion with my correct environment —*
Internal Markets — the results didn't just shift how I felt day-to-day. They showed up in something bigger: the reversal of my biological age.

29

Environment: Where You're Meant to Thrive

If **Digestion** shows you how your body takes in nourishment, **Environment** shows you where your body is designed to thrive.

This isn't about paint colors, feng shui, or aesthetic preference. Environment in Human Design is biological. It tells you the kinds of spaces that regulate your system, reduce stress, and help your body regenerate. When you spend time in your correct environment, your digestion improves, your sleep deepens, your focus sharpens—and yes, you can even slow or reverse aging.

Environment is revealed through the lower-left arrow in your chart. There are six archetypes, but each has both an Active (Left) and Passive (Right) expression—making 12 distinct environment types in total.

The 12 Human Design Environments

1 & 2. Caves

- **Active Caves:** Thrive in secure, controlled spaces where they decide who and what comes in.
- **Passive Caves:** Still need safety, but in a less rigid way. Thrive when others come to them and they filter interactions on their terms.

3 & 4. Markets

- **Active (External) Markets:** Thrive in bustling spaces of exchange—goods, ideas, energy. The buzz stimulates them.
- **Passive (Internal) Markets:** Prefer curated, selective hubs. Contained spaces where they can choose their exchanges.

5 & 6. Kitchens (Laboratories)

- **Active Kitchens:** Thrive in environments of transformation—literal kitchens, labs, or workshops. They want to actively stir the pot.
- **Passive Kitchens:** Nourished simply by being in spaces where transformation is happening, even if they're not the one leading it.

7 & 8. Mountains

- **Active Mountains:** Thrive in elevated spaces with perspective and stimulation—physically higher or energetically "above the fray."
- **Passive Mountains:** Prefer more removed elevation—quiet, remote, or undisturbed higher ground.

9 & 10. Valleys

- **Active Valleys:** Thrive in open, low spaces with constant communication flow. They need to engage actively.
- **Passive Valleys:** Prefer to listen, observe, and absorb information. Still nourished by the flow, but more as receivers.

11 & 12. Shores

- **Active Shores:** Thrive in transitional zones—edges between two worlds, like beaches or city borders. They need movement and change.
- **Passive Shores:** Prefer to observe transitions without diving into them. Just being near the "in-between" is enough.

My Environment: Internal Markets

I'm a **Markets person—specifically Internal Markets.** That means I thrive in curated exchange hubs where I can choose my interactions.

Not the chaos of outdoor festivals. You will never find me at a Farmers Market. My body and energy work best in **contained, selective spaces** where there's flow, but also order.

Once I learned this, everything clicked.

- Loud, open-plan offices drained me.
- A remote peaceful hut left me uninspired.
- Food truck events in a parking lot could bore me.

So I started making intentional changes:

- Choosing co-working spaces with phone booths or coffee shops.
- Doing house calls.
- Creating a "markets vibe" in my living space—beautiful, contained, curated.

The result? My energy came back. I wasn't fighting my environment anymore. My body could finally relax into its design.

```
Why Environment Matters for Biohacking
You can follow the "perfect" diet, stack the right
supplements, and buy the most expensive red light
panel--but if you're living in the wrong
environment, your biology is still swimming upstream.
 Correct environment = less stress, better
 digestion, deeper rest.
```

```
Wrong environment = silent resistance that
accelerates aging.
```

How to Start Your Environment Experiment

If you don't know your Environment Type, you can book a session with me to run your chart using the official Maia Mechanics software. You can also schedule a reading with a certified analyst who specializes in Variable Readings (the four arrows).

Sure, you *could* take a risk and use an unverified AI app or Google it — but make sure you have your exact birth time. Trust me: I learned the hard (and expensive) way that even a slightly wrong birth time can completely change your Variables.

Once you know your correct Environment, start observing:

· Which spaces leave you feeling energized, focused, and alive?
· Which ones leave you foggy, drained, or irritable?
· How can you shift even 10–20% more of your time into the correct environment?

You don't have to sell your house or move across the world overnight. A fun start is to intentionally choose where you vacation next and see if you notice anything. Small, intentional adjustments add up. Sometimes the biggest biohack is simply putting your body in the place where it's wired to thrive.

Why This Matters for Biohacking

You can have the perfect meal timing, the best supplements, and the cleanest eating habits... but if you're in the wrong environment, your body still suffers. Stress hormones stay high. Recovery slows. Sleep tanks. Your "anti-aging" efforts start feeling like swimming upstream. You may not be aware of this until you intentionally try to stay in your Human Design advanced chart "environment" type. The difference could really surprise you.

When I started tracking this, I realized my energy crashes were almost always tied to:

- Being in environments that weren't "Internal Market" friendly.
- Staying too long in someone else's aura — especially sacral beings (hello, Generators) — and forgetting to come back to my own energetic baseline.
- Going on vacation to the mountains, was boring and not rejuvenating.

Once I saw the pattern, I started biohacking my environment just like my food:

- Leaving events before the "social hangover" hit.
- Scheduling recovery days after high-interaction weeks.
- Saying "yes" to one-on-one dinners and "no" to chaotic group outings.

```
Experiment Invitation
Try this: for the next 7 days, track how you feel
before, during, and after being in different
environments. Note your mood, focus, appetite, and
energy levels. Look for patterns.
You might be shocked at how much your environment
impacts your biology -- sometimes even more than the
"big" biohacks you've tried.
```

We've now covered how you eat (Digestion) and where you thrive (Environment) — the two biggest levers for your biology. Next, let's enjoy some real life stories and applications, let the entertainment begin.

VI

Stories & Biohacking Applications

30

I'm a Cheeky Bitch — Literally and Figuratively

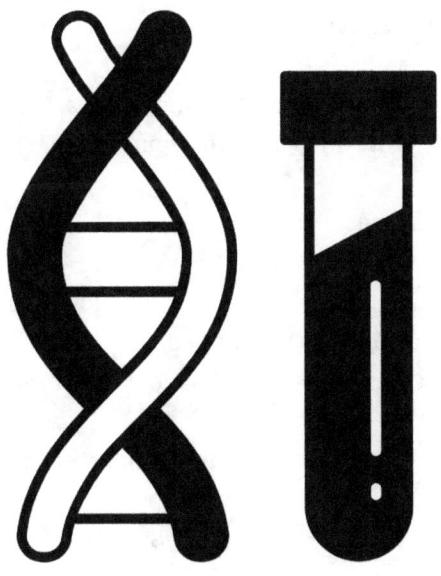

Let's talk cheeks — because mine, thanks to Tally Health, have been busy proving that you can turn back time.

Tally Health tracks biological age using a simple cheek swab. It measures key biomarkers to reveal how "young" or "old" your body actually is compared to your chronological age. It's not vanity data — it's insight into longevity, cellular health, and how your lifestyle choices are truly landing in your body.

My Wake-Up Call

When my first results came in, I was stunned:

My biological age was older than my real age.

How could that be?

I was sober, mindful, eating clean, sleeping well, laughing often, detoxing my home, and working with hormone special-ists. By all appearances, I was doing everything "right."

But data doesn't lie. And those results were my wake-up call.

Over the next 1 year, 2 months, and 22 days, I got biologically younger — 3 years and 3 months younger, to be exact.

Bio-Age Timeline

- March 7, 2023: 18 months older biologically than my chronological age. (Yes, I cried.)
- June 7, 2023: Only 3 months older → 15 months younger in 3 months.
- October 7, 2023: 2 months younger → 5 more months gained.
- December 6, 2023: 12 months younger → 10 more months gained.
- March 6, 2024: 30 months (2.5 years) younger → another

big leap.

- May 29, 2024: 21 months younger → a small backslide, 9 months lost.

Progress, not perfection.

The Real Turning Point

That initial Tally result cracked me open.

It didn't make sense — my habits looked healthy, but my DNA methylation markers told another story. So when a client gifted me her ticket to the Biohacking Conference in Beverly Hills, I said hell yes.

The first talk was pure ego theater — puffed-up alpha energy in designer sneakers — but one line hit me between the eyes:

"You have to know your genetic blueprint before you can even begin this journey."

Here I was, someone obsessed with individuality and energetic blueprints through Human Design — yet I hadn't done a DNA test. It wasn't neglect, just timing. I was finally ready.

DNA

While wandering the Hilton ballroom filled with cryotherapy pods and peptide pushers, I found my match: a DNA testing company with deep data and clinician pricing. I signed up on the spot.

Weeks later, my report landed with more precision than any horoscope or wellness quiz ever could. Charts, graphs, and personalized voice notes decoded everything from mood to micronutrients:

- **Mood & Behavior**: Addiction risks, anxiety, procrastination, burnout tendencies.
- **Diet & Nutrition:** How my genes handle carbs, fats, and

micronutrient absorption.

· **Lifestyle Factors:** Sleep quality, circadian rhythm, and stress resilience.

· **Hormones, Fitness & Longevity**: Recovery needs, inflammation, cardiovascular markers, and aging potential.

It wasn't perfect — some parts were obvious or oversimplified — but overall, it was revolutionary. For the first time, I saw how Human Design, genetics, and biohacking could merge into one personalized operating system.

Blood, Saliva & Biohacking

Blood Testing:

Quarterly blood panels provide comprehensive data on physiological and metabolic health markers, including hormone levels (such as cortisol, thyroid, sex hormones), lipid profile (cholesterol fractions), glycemic control (glucose, HbA1c), liver and kidney function, and markers of systemic inflammation. These tests offer critical insights into organ function, endocrine balance, and disease risk.

Saliva Testing:

Saliva tests are used primarily for non-invasive monitoring of biochemical and molecular biomarkers. This includes measurements of nitric oxide levels, which reflect vascular and endothelial function, as well as epigenetic analyses like DNA methylation profiling to assess biological age and cellular aging processes.

```
Integrated Approach:
Combining serum blood analysis with saliva-based
molecular testing establishes a robust feedback
system for precision biohacking. Blood tests
```

```
quantify current systemic function and nutrient
status, while saliva tests provide dynamic
information on cellular aging and adaptive
responses. This integrative biomarker approach
enables targeted interventions optimizing longevity
and personalized health strategies.
```

Meat

My DNA results also gave me permission to listen to what my body already knew: meat works for me.

I grew up on a Minnesota farm surrounded by cows, pigs, chickens, and cornfields. For us, meat wasn't indulgence — it was fuel. So when my blood type came back as O, and I re-read Eat Right for Your Blood Type, I felt vindicated.

Around the same time, I dove into Dr. Paul Saladino's research on nose-to-tail eating and nutrient density. Goodbye salad guilt. Hello liver capsules. Even my sister Heather's dip into Asian constitutional medicine confirmed I struggle with rough fibers and raw veggies. Kale and cabbage made me bloated; steak made me sparkle.

Now, when I tell people I'm "allergic to vegetables," they laugh — but I'm only half kidding. (Carrot cake remains the sacred exception: the only vegetable that's never betrayed me.)

What Actually Made Me Younger

Supplements and science helped — but alignment changed everything.

TallyHealth's formulas gave me a foundation:

Vitality: alpha-ketoglutarate, quercetin, resveratrol, fisetin, spermidine.

Amplify: glycine, berberine, CoQ10.

Then I customized based on my DNA results, layering in nutrients matched to my genetic blueprint. But the biggest biological age reversal came from living my design.

- **Following My Human Design**: As a Projector, I worked less, rested more, and only said yes when my willpower aligned.

- **Movement:** Biking daily, lifting weights 5–7 times a week, and saltwater swims.
- **Socializing:** Dating, new friendships, dinners out — community as medicine.
- **Coworking:** My "Internal Markets" thrive in lively indoor spaces, so co-working cafés became my biohacking cheat code.
- **Emotional Freedom:** Years of therapy, applied. Sometimes messy, sometimes magical, always honest.
- **Mindset**: NLP training, meditation, and long, reflective ocean floats.
- **Diet & Fasting**: High-protein, low-carb, intermittent fasting, minimal sugar, no alcohol.
- **Money & Stability**: Lean finances, smarter savings, sustainable goals.
- **Spiritual Simplicity:** Yoga, meditation circles, breathwork, and quiet joy at home.
- **Self-Love**: Compassion, curiosity, and a very healthy solo sex life (thank you, nervous system regulation).

When everything — my lifestyle, work rhythm, relationships, finances, and Human Design strategy — came into coherence, that's when rejuvenation happened. It wasn't magic. It was alignment.

The Fork in the Road

My DNA, saliva, and blood told the same truth: my body was asking for a new kind of care.

So I listened — to the science, to my design, to my intuition. That was the moment I stopped guessing and started intelligent biohacking — grounded in data, aligned with energy, and sprinkled with cheeky rebellion.

And from there, the story only gets wilder. Because while I got younger in the lab, I also got funnier on stage. Coming up next: Doing a Lot of Comedy, Not Much Biohacking.

31

Biohacking Meets Comedy

Fearless on stage, sloppy at the dinner table.

When I started stand-up comedy, I dove in headfirst — fearless, over-caffeinated, and operating like a Generator instead of the Projector that I am. Comedy club menus are not designed for longevity: greasy wings, deep-fried chicken strips, nachos, and enough Red Bull to fuel a rave. If there was a "salad" option, it usually looked like garnish for the chicken tenders.

The toll on my body was real. Late nights, traffic, skipped workouts, and bar food between open mics — all while I was trying to build a career on stage. Looking back, it's no wonder I didn't see visible "youth gains" in my biological age during that time.

But comedy isn't just about bad food and worse sleep. It's about fear. Every set was a test: writing new jokes, bombing at open mics, sweating under stage lights, praying no one uploaded my class-show disasters to YouTube. Comedy became a two-year immersion in facing fear — and that, I now realize, is its own form of biohacking.

The Hustle: From Dive Bars to International Shows

Despite not living "in alignment," I hustled like my life depended on it. In two years, I performed everywhere:

- Dive bars, comedy clubs, and festivals across Los Angeles, Austin, London, Cambridge, Chicago, Phoenix, San Diego, Las Vegas, and Santa Barbara.
- Open mics at *The Comedy Store, Laugh Factory, Flappers, Wiseguys* (yes, Pauly Shore's club).
- Pandemic-era Zoom shows (aka the most soul-sucking form of comedy).

- International gigs in England, and even headlining in Santa Barbara.

I treated comedy like a business — networking, booking, traveling — and yes, pushing myself beyond what's sustainable for a Projector. People called me "lucky." It wasn't luck. It was grind.

The saving grace? My comedy buddy, Gini Sikes. After every show, good or bad, she found something kind to say. Every comic needs a Gini.

Biohacking Meets Comedy: The Mindset Factor

From a biohacking lens, comedy was terrible for my biology. My digestion, sleep, and recovery all tanked. But my *mindset*? That actually improved. Facing fear night after night — bombing, killing, and everything in between — rewired me in ways no supplement could. Humor healed me. Laughter really was medicine.

By my second year of comedy, I ran another Tally Health cheek swab. Despite my late-night pizza runs and questionable gas-station snacks, my biological age had actually dropped (got slightly younger). Apparently, mindset really does move the needle.

But let's be real: mindset isn't everything. Watch early videos of me on stage and you'll see the truth. Not just in the jokes (some were rough), but in how I held myself — trying to suck in my belly fat while making strangers laugh. Comedy taught me resilience, but it also reminded me that no hack works if you're living out of alignment with your design.

Laughter as a Biohack

Stress reduction: Comedy floods your body with endorphins.

Resilience training: Facing fear repeatedly builds tolerance to stress.

Longevity factor: Humor improves mood, relationships, and mental health -- all linked to slower aging.

32

Is Chrissy Snow Your Hero Too?

Growing up, I watched *Three's Company*, and of course, Chrissy Snow was the quintessential ditzy blonde. She made me laugh, but I didn't exactly look up to her. Years later, I discovered that Suzanne Somers—the actress who played Chrissy—was actually one of the earliest female pioneers in biohacking and hormone optimization. Suddenly, being a Chrissy Snow fan felt like being part of a secret sisterhood.

At the time, I was working in a plastic surgeon's office where hormone replacement therapy was offered to celebrity clients. The doctor's wife—who was my age—looked at least 15 years younger. That lit a fire under me. I wanted to know *everything* about anti-aging, biohacking, and hormone replacement therapy.

Not long after, I took a job as an esthetician at another hormone doctor's office in Santa Monica, CA. His wife was also a hormone specialist, and their waiting room was basically a shrine to Suzanne Somers' books. She had interviewed top doctors, compiled their wisdom, and made hormone health accessible to everyday women.

Suzanne didn't just accept the medical status quo—she asked hard questions, experimented on herself, and shared what worked. Her books were empowering and unflinchingly practical. I found my hormone doctor through her website.

My Menopause Wake-Up Call

At that time, I was still getting my period regularly, but I couldn't help but notice how some women seemed to breeze through menopause while others struggled visibly. I read about women in Peru consuming maca root daily and experiencing fewer symptoms. I may have been concerned about menopause earlier than necessary, but I wanted to get ahead of it.

Hot flashes eventually arrived—mostly at night—and I knew I needed a plan. I found Dr. Allen Peters through Suzanne Somers' network and started bioidentical hormone replacement therapy under his care. His wife, Jeanne, became my nutritionist, and together they monitored my hormones with quarterly blood tests.

Their approach was integrative, progressive, and data-driven. They were adamant about avoiding synthetic hormones, and they didn't just preach health—they lived it. I was surrounded by people who made aging look *optional*. I was impatient but they were very encouraging and my consistency finally began to show results. Thank you Jeanne and Dr Peters.

The result? I got my energy back. My mood stabilized. My body felt like it belonged to me again. And most importantly, I didn't just survive menopause—I thrived.

```
Biohacking Lesson from Suzanne Somers
Don't wait for your health to hit a crisis point
before seeking answers. Get curious early.
Ask questions. Run labs. Surround yourself with
people who look like your future self.
```

This deepened my realization that aging could be hacked—not with denial, but with data, science, and a little bit of audacity. And that realization would shape every decision I made on my biohacking journey—from what I ate to where I lived to how I laughed my way through the challenges of stand-up comedy.

33

I'm in Miami, Bitch - But First, Mold and Stalkers

Carlos, my fellow comedian, had the most piercingly dark blue eyes I'd ever seen—set against rich brown skin. I was performing at a dive bar comedy show he was hosting, and I couldn't resist asking:

"What's your ethnicity? I've never seen dark blue eyes and dark skin on an Earthling before."

He laughed and told me his story: years earlier, he'd almost gone blind from black mold poisoning. That experience, strangely enough, changed the color of his eyes.

His story hit me hard—and not just because of the eye thing.

At the time, I had a habit of storing my boots in plastic bins under my bed during California summers. I didn't need them often, but when I pulled them out, I'd wipe the green mold off with vinegar and lemon. After talking to Carlos, something clicked. I inspected my apartment and—yep—black mold on the windowsills. Instant panic.

I put on a mask, scrubbed everything with vinegar and lemon, then nuked it with bleach. I wasn't about to mess with fate—or my vision.

Thankfully, my two young landlords actually cared. They replaced the windows, remediated the mold, and even put me up in a hotel for a two nights. California tenant laws can be brutal for landlords, but they were a blessing for me— especially compared to Florida's. (But that's another story.)

The Florida Detour

While all this was unfolding, I was spending hours each night on the phone with a man I'd met in a David R. Hawkins spiritual Zoom group. Sober. Spiritual. Dreamy blue eyes. A possible romantic match—or so I thought.

I needed a break from LA's post-COVID anxiety, and Florida always gave me life. So I booked an 11-day trip—Airbnb, beach plans, art galleries, the works. I told myself it was a mini-experiment: pretending I already lived the Florida lifestyle.

After the mold drama and hotel stay, I flew straight from LA to Hollywood, FL. Looking back, that should've been my moment to move to Florida permanently. Mold was the perfect excuse to break my lease. But I was still the "good girl" who didn't want to rock the boat. Typical 3/5 in Human Design: trial and error—emphasis on error.

Anyway, I went. I lived. I learned.

The man? A total disaster. He smoked a pack of cigarettes a day, lived in a hotel, hadn't been tested for STDs after his HIV-positive ex girlfriend, and couldn't get it up. Spiritual, yes—but also limp, toxic, and terrifying.

After that bombshell, I bolted. I ended up on the Florida expressway without a SunPass, crying at the beach— overwhelmed and disoriented. That was Day Two of my "vacation." And to top it off, he later became a stalker— sending me 65 emails in one day and even creeping on my Alignable account. (Spiritual predator is the new term I think)

I changed my location on Alignable to Chelsea, NY just to mess with him. Predictably, that triggered another flood of messages.

In hindsight that vacation was multifaceted as I'll share more about in a second, but the man, did not 'recognize' and 'invite' me, as a Projector is encouraged to live.

The Aura Shock Factor

Now let's talk about the real Human Design plot twist: aura shock.

As a Projector with the Right Angle Cross of Penetration and the Channel of Shock, my energy isn't just present— it's penetrating. Apparently, my aura comes with its own disclaimer: handle with care.

Some call it "magnetic." My friends call it magic—maybe dangerously so.

Let's just say my love life has had unforgettable moments. My first boyfriend jumped out of a two-story window, declaring he couldn't live without me (he limped away with only a twisted ankle and, presumably, a new respect for gravity and regret). My second boyfriend's story was far darker—he died by suicide. That loss rocked me, and honoring his memory has been a huge part of my healing. His mother later shared that he struggled deeply with depression, which brought a new layer of tenderness and understanding to our history.

Yes—the "auric essence" is real, but unchecked magic can leave a trail of wild stories and lessons. Two stalkers, two tragic romances, and years of self-study later, I've realized my energy requires discernment, boundaries, and a dash of spiritual jiu-jitsu.

And here's where comedy enters the chat. In stand-up, we're taught to mine our complaints—aka, channel your drama for laughs. My crew of female comics had a hilarious ongoing bit about women's secret power, calling it our "Magic P*ssy"—MP for short. The guys on the circuit were completely bewildered. We'd casually drop, "MP this, MP that," and watch them try to decode the mystery. Sometimes, ladies, not sharing your magic is actually an act of mercy.

Honestly, a lot of men unconsciously know they can't handle the potency—they sense the hurricane and wisely decide not to upgrade their emotional infrastructure. If a man doesn't pick you? Don't take it personally, goddess. Sometimes respecting your magic means letting go, knowing it wasn't meant to be.

Because with all magic—auric, comic, or otherwise—comes great responsibility. And sometimes that responsibility is keeping your legendary energy on a need-to-know basis.

Comedy as Medicine

After the heartbreak, the mold scare, and sitting in that

Hollywood, FL Airbnb, I went into full "f*ck-it" mode. I was terrified I had HIV and started checking off my bucket list. Stand-up comedy had been on there for years.

I called a friend back in LA for a comedy coach recommendation, audited a Zoom class for free, dropped punchlines in the chat—and to my surprise, the coach read them out loud, laughed, and I felt seen, respected, alive.

That moment was medicine.

The next day, I booked a reading with Rosie Cutter, a Human Design and Destiny Card reader I'd followed online. I asked, "Could everything in my chart play out if I pursued stand-up?" She lit up and said yes. She tied every element of my reading back to comedy, validating something I hadn't dared to claim: I was meant to do this.

My chart said it all—Projector. Penetrating aura. Channel of Shock. Right Angle Cross of Penetration. Shocking and penetrating? That's literally the definition of a comic.

So, I dove in. I studied, performed, wrote, and pursued comedy full-time for nearly two years, as I mentioned earlier. And you know what? I felt free. I was healing through humor, shocking people into awareness, and finally living my design. It was a leveled-up alignment—palpable and powerful. I just wish it was financially profitable. Oh well, wealth has many metrics.

Why This Story Matters

This chapter might feel like a side quest, but it's not. It's about deconditioning through chaos. It's about how trauma, comedy, and identity collide. It's about recognizing your energetic power—and learning to wield it with awareness.

This Florida trip was a turning point. It was the messy

middle between life deep in Human Design experimentation and life fully aligned with it. And while I didn't move then, I eventually did. Looking back, I think I had to collect more pain before I could muster the will to act—probably a learning curve of having my Heart/Will Center as my Inner Authority.

So yeah, I'm in Miami, bitch, for a long visit, should have stayed, but will be back later.

34

I'm in Miami, Bitch - Finally

In 2023, I packed my life into boxes and made a cross-country leap from Los Angeles to Miami. It wasn't just a relocation — it was a full energetic reset. I wanted more than a new zip code. I wanted a new nervous system and to keep getting younger.

Miami was loud, unapologetic, alive. The city matched my Internal Markets Environment — curated exchange, high-end spaces, buzzing energy. There was a rhythm to Miami that woke me up in a way Los Angeles never did, plus the ocean is clean and warm all year round.

But Miami also challenged me. The humidity, the heat, the sheer sensory input — it was a lot. So, I doubled down on my biohacking practices. Blackout curtains went up in the bedroom. I scheduled my days to match my Indirect Light digestion. I found boutique gyms, high-end grocery stores, and coworking hubs that felt like curated "markets."

Somewhere in the middle of it all, a friend called me "a cheeky bitch." Not as an insult — as a compliment. "You're gutsy," she said. "You speak your mind. You're not trying to blend in."

She was right. Miami gave me permission to be louder, to take up space, to be unapologetically myself. My business evolved, my coaching practice deepened, and my body started responding — faster recovery, better sleep, better labs.

```
Biohacking Your Move
If your environment is wrong, no supplement stack
will save you.
Moving cities isn't always the answer -- but
adjusting your environment is.
Ask yourself: do I feel more alive where I am... or
am I constantly recovering from where I live?
```

Miami wasn't just a move. It was a rebrand — of my business, my biology, and my identity. I became more visible, more magnetic, and yes — cheekier.

35

Coffee: My Morning Ritual

My love affair with coffee began in my early 20s. This legal "drug" quickly became my companion — never judging me, always there to fuel me through the day. What started as a simple caffeine fix evolved into one of the main staples of my biohacking routine — and one of the most sacred parts of my day.

As of 2025, my morning coffee recipe is a carefully crafted ritual. I start with organic, fair-trade beans — half-caffeinated and half-decaf, so it's essentially a half-caff brew.

My First Cup Includes:

- Grass-fed, unsalted butter
- Organic bovine collagen powder
- Organic stevia
- Organic cinnamon and turmeric (with a pinch of black pepper to activate the turmeric)
- Mushroom master blend
- Organic half-and-half or heavy whipping cream (preferably pasteurized, not ultra-pasteurized)

This isn't just "coffee" — this is fuel. I see it as part of my morning ritual, designed to nourish my body in a way that supports my biohacking goals. It's a custom routine for me, but I wouldn't recommend it to everyone.

What Brain-Fuel Coffee Really Is

For those who haven't heard of this concept, brain-fuel coffee (sometimes branded elsewhere) is a high-calorie coffee drink made with brewed coffee, unsalted butter, and medium-chain triglyceride (MCT) oil. It's blended to create a creamy texture and is designed to provide sustained energy and mental clarity, often used as a meal replacement in low-carb or ketogenic diets. The combination of healthy fats from the butter and MCT oil is believed to enhance cognitive function and promote fat burning.

Over time, I've made this recipe my own — swapping cinnamon for cassia, experimenting with organic cassia essential oil, and in the fall, adding pumpkin pie spice for a seasonal twist. My first cup has become a golden-milk-meets-coffee mashup — warm, spicy, and energizing.

The Second Cup

In the late morning, I enjoy a second half-caff cup, which includes:

- Organic stevia
- Organic collagen powder
- Ashwagandha powder (a tiny bit)
- Organic cacao
- Organic creamer
- Organic Maca

This keeps me sharp and sustains me until I naturally break my fast later in the day (a nod to my Indirect Light Digestion type).

My Biohacking Rules for Coffee

Currently, I limit my caffeine intake to two half-caff cups a day and avoid caffeine after 2 PM. But like any good experimenter, I expect this routine to evolve as my biohacking journey continues — because I fully admit it: I have a love affair with coffee, and I like my coffee to be sexy.

If you decide to try this, get a good milk frother or whisk to blend everything well. Mushrooms, collagen, and turmeric can settle at the bottom if left to sit, so whisk or stir occasionally.

Quick confession, since I've been deep into writing and editing this book I have visited Japan and now I have added an early afternoon Matcha Latte. Organic Matcha green tea powder, whisk like crazy and then add stevia, organic half and half. Hopefully with the half caff coffee's and the Matcha you'll see this book for sale by November.

```
Biohacking Tip
Coffee as a Ritual, Not Just a Drink:
 When coffee becomes part of a mindful routine --
 instead of a frantic grab-and-go fix -- it can
 anchor your morning, support your digestion, and
 set your day up with clarity and intention. Track
 how different coffee styles, blends, and timing
 affect your energy, mood, and sleep. The right
 coffee, at the right time, can be a biohack.
 Especially for Projectors, Manifestors and
 Reflectors, because we don't have that motor the
 Sacral center defined in our charts.
```

I invite you to experiment, savor, and truly enjoy your coffee — just as I do. Thank you, Mother Nature, for this incredible plant medicine. I am forever grateful.

36

Save Your Money: Getting Old Is Expensive

Let's be honest: aging is expensive. And not cute expensive—like a vintage Chanel bag or a bougie Beverly Hills green juice. I mean the kind of expensive where you silently hemorrhage money just to keep your body from falling apart.

Nobody warned me about this. Why aren't we taught real life skills in school—like how to file taxes, pick a decent health plan, or negotiate a medical bill? Instead, we all piece things together from TikTok, trauma, and unsolicited advice from strangers in the Whole Foods checkout line.

I've had to pick up financial survival skills like Indiana Jones dodging booby traps—mostly by catching subtle clues that "looking good" and "feeling good" both come with a price tag.

The House Hustle Trap

If you're self-employed or freelance, everyone loves to tell you to report all your income so you look "responsible" to the bank. Then the bank gives you a giant mortgage, and suddenly you "own" a home. Except you don't—the bank does. And now you're chained to a loan, your health insurance premiums skyrocket, and you're paying for repairs like you're running a nonprofit renovation project. (All of this is my opinion, not financial advice)

Health Insurance Reality Check

When I lived in Florida, I paid $6.02/month for health insurance. Yes, six dollars. Later, after reporting more income? My premium jumped to $848.07/month. Why? Because some algorithm decided that once you cross 50, you're statistically doomed to chronic illness and expensive meds.

But what if you're a healthy biohacker who just wants coverage in case of a rogue paddleboard accident or a scooter taking you out on Lincoln Road? The math doesn't work. The system punishes health-conscious adults for not being sick enough to justify the premiums. WTF?

Hormone Highway Robbery

Don't get me started on labs. The ones insurance will cover are designed for 30-year-old men worried about cholesterol—not 50 something-year-old women optimizing hormone levels so we don't cry over paper towels in Target. Want relevant labs? You'll need to request them specifically, argue with your doctor, and then pay out of pocket anyway.

And once you cross into perimenopause or menopause, hormone replacement therapy becomes essential—but only if you don't want your endocrine system confused by cheap synthetic knockoffs. Compounded bioidentical hormones are the gold standard—and guess what? Insurance doesn't cover them. No real healthy biohacker would put synthetic hormones in their body.

Big Picture, Babe

All this to say: aging + biohacking = expensive AF. And no one tells you this until you're knee-deep in lab bills, supplements, and boutique recovery sessions wondering why your credit card statement looks like a Goop starter kit.

But here's the reframe: your health is your highest-yield investment. Every dollar you spend on aligning your biology—whether that's hormones, supplements, or finally getting your environment and digestion right—is money that pays you back in vitality, clarity, and years of life.

Because the truth is, you are the asset. Keeping you thriving isn't optional. It's strategy. But the reason I mentioned all of this is so you 30 year olds can get a dose of reality, and start a health savings account for yourself, NOW. You'll be glad you did.

37

The Journey Began Under the Kitchen Sink

My biohacking journey began with a simple but powerful shift: **rethinking the products I used in my home**.

It started in 2016 when my sister Heather, a health coach, introduced me to the idea of **environmental toxins** and their impact on the body. She had already been deep into the research, and during a conversation at **Expo West in Anaheim, California**, something clicked for me.

She inspired me—I needed to take action. So I hired her as my health coach.

The Tools That Changed Everything

We both began using the **Environmental Working Group (EWG)** website to evaluate everything from cleaning products to personal care items. Their **"Skin Deep"** database became our go-to tool.

By scanning product barcodes with our phones, we could instantly see how toxic a product was, based on a score from **zero to ten**.

- A **zero** meant "safe."
- Anything above a 2 or 3, raised **red flags**.

I became particularly obsessed with identifying **hormone and endocrine disruptors**—chemicals that mess with your body's hormonal balance—because I knew I needed to protect myself from anything that could quietly sabotage my health.

He Was Right: A Sea of Poison

The deeper I went, the more I realized just how toxic our environment really is.

As **Dr. Mark Hyman** says, we live in a:

"**Sea of poison**"—a bleak truth, but a true one.

Suddenly, the things I had never questioned—like **deodorant**, **toothpaste**, and even my favorite **body lotion**—started to look like villains in disguise.

Ingredients like:

· **Partially hydrogenated oils**
· **Synthetic colorants** (hello, Yellow #5)
· **Parabens**

...became red flags I could no longer ignore.

Home Detox: Room by Room
Step 1: The Kitchen Sink

Determined to make better choices, I taught myself how to **read labels** and **spot sneaky toxins**.

Products I once thought were "safe" turned out to be anything but.

With the help of the EWG and other research tools, I began **scrutinizing every product** in my home.

If something had a **high toxicity score**—or worse, contained known **hormone disruptors**—it went straight in the trash.

The phrase **"hormone disruptor"** practically jumped off the page at me.

As a woman, I wanted my hormones working **for me**, not **against me**.

I couldn't un-know what I'd learned, and I refused to pretend it didn't matter.

Step 2: The Bathroom

- **Windex?** Gone.
- That **fancy lotion?** Tossed.

If it had **artificial fragrance**, **synthetic dye**, or any other **red-flag chemical**, it didn't make the cut.

I even dove into **ingredient research**, discovering the long-term effects of additives like **Red #6**.

It was overwhelming, yes—but also **empowering**.

Knowledge gave me agency.

The DIY Era Begins

Heather and I also began experimenting with **DIY alternatives**.

Over the next few years, I took on the challenge of making my own personal care products:

- Toothpaste
- Dry shampoo
- Face powder
- Deodorant

Using ingredients like:

- **Coconut oil**
- Organic Cacao powder
- **Arrowroot powder**
- **Essential oils**

...I created simple formulas that felt cleaner and safer.

Was it perfect? No. But it was **intentional**, and that felt like a win.

A New Way of Living

As I learned more, I realized this wasn't just about **purging toxic products**—it was about **creating a new way of living**.

- I started using a **vinegar-and-lemon essential oil spray** to clean my windows.
- I kept the same **reusable hand soap bottle** for three years. Because I care about mother earth.

Detoxing my home naturally led me toward a **simpler**, more **sustainable** lifestyle—one with:

- **Less plastic**
- **Fewer chemicals**
- And way more **peace of mind**

The Fear of Staying Ignorant

Let's be honest:

It wasn't easy, and it wasn't quick.

The **fear of staying ignorant** haunted me.

I didn't want to keep unknowingly exposing myself to chemicals I couldn't even pronounce.

At some point, I had to face the truth and take back control.

That's when I realized:

Informed awareness is the first step in any real biohacking journey.

Start Here: Your Home Audit Challenge

That's why I'm sharing this with you—so you can skip the **years of trial and error** and start with **awareness**.

```
I challenge you to do a home audit.
Start in your kitchen.
 Toss anything with synthetic fragrance or
 artificial dye.
Then go into your bathroom.
 Look for parabens, phthalates, or other toxic
 ingredients.
 If you find them? Ditch them.
```

These chemicals have **no business in your body**. Ideally empty the plastic bottles, rinse them and recycle properly. (Maybe in a follow up blog we'll discuss more about plastics. Or a podcast interview.)

Use the Tools, Build the Skills

If you're ready to go deeper, use the **EWG database** to scan barcodes and see how your current products rank. I've also heard Yuka app is pretty good, but I haven't heard great reviews about ingred.io, yet. Do your research.

You don't have to become an expert overnight—

but over time, you'll build a **skill set** that makes choosing safer products **second nature**.

Your Home Is Your Sanctuary

Creating a **cleaner, safer home** is the gateway to **biohacking your environment**.

At the end of the day, your home should be your:

· **Sanctuary**
· **Space for rest**
· **Place of healing**

· **Hub of restoration**

When you take the time to evaluate what you bring into that space,
you're not just avoiding toxins—
You're investing in your long-term health and well-being.

So... How Many Grocery Bags of Toxins Are Hiding in Your Cabinets?
This is your **starting point**.
This is how your **biohacking journey begins**—
with **awareness**, **choice**, and the **courage to do things differently**.
Say **bye-bye** to all those **hotel samples** you've taken home over the years.
You don't need them.
You've got something better now: **clarity**.

38

Mother Nature: Your Free Biohack

Forget the fancy biohacks for a moment — one of the most powerful tools for your health is free and always available: nature.

Walking barefoot in grass, putting your feet in the sand, or swimming in the ocean exposes you to **negative ions** — charged particles that can literally shift your biology.

Why Negative Ions Matter

Negative ions are found in abundance near water, forests, and natural environments. When you connect with them, your body responds in profound ways:

- **Improved Mood & Mental Clarity** — Negative ions increase oxygen flow to the brain, which can reduce stress and boost focus.
- **Immune Boosting** — Regular exposure strengthens your immune system, helping you fight off illness.
- **Better Sleep** — They help balance serotonin levels, leading to deeper, more restorative sleep.
- **Energy Reset** — A beach walk or barefoot moment can leave you feeling like you just had an emotional tune-up.
- **Allergy & Respiratory Relief** — They help clear dust, pollen, and other irritants from the air.

This isn't just woo — there's science behind why we feel calmer after a walk by the ocean or standing under a waterfall.

My Experience as an "Indirect Light" Type

Because I'm an **Indirect Light digestion type**, the beach isn't where I do my best thinking or working. Direct sunlight shuts down my appetite and scrambles my focus — I can't even read a book on the sand. Instead of being mentally sharp, I slip into total relaxation. And when I'm that relaxed, I'm honestly not much of a conversationalist.

If I go to the beach with a friend, we usually end up with long stretches of silence — not in a bad way, just... solar-induced quiet. My real girlfriend bonding happens elsewhere: tucked into a dark corner of a coffee shop, where my mind and my energy are both fully alive.

But barefoot grounding? That works for me — even if I do it in the shade. I get the benefit of negative ions without fighting my natural rhythm.

A Simple (and Free) Biohacking Ritual

Next time you're stressed, foggy, or just "off," try this:

- Take off your shoes and stand barefoot on grass or sand for 10–15 minutes.
- Or dip your feet into the ocean, a lake, or even a bathtub of warm water with sea salt.
- If you can, sit still — let your breath slow, and notice how your body starts to shift.

You might be surprised how much you can reset without spending a dollar.

VII

Relationships, Breakthroughs & Empowerment

39

Dating by Design: Love, Invitations, and Saying No

Each Human Design Type has a unique Signature — a state of well-being that signals you're living in alignment with your design. Earlier in the book, I called this the pendulum—an inner compass you can access to make quick, aligned decisions. Your Signature is like a "yes" light going on when you're on the right track, and a "no" warning when you're not. (You may want to review chapter 15)

Equally important is acknowledging that each Type carries a distinct Aura—an energetic field that communicates before you even say a word. Your aura broadcasts your energy and influences how others perceive and respond to you. Understanding your aura helps you navigate relationships, especially dating, with greater ease and authenticity. (You may want to review chapters 8 & 9)

Lastly, every Type has a specific Strategy—a reliable pathway to interact with the world and make decisions. Remembering and honoring your Strategy not only brings you closer to your Signature but also optimizes how you connect with others romantically and socially. (You may want to review chapter 16)

The Types and Their Key Energetic Tools

- **Manifestors:** Signature is peace. Strategy is to inform others before acting. Their aura is a powerful initiating force that impacts others energetically. In dating, Manifestors thrive when clear about intentions and giving partners space to respond.
- **Generators (including Manifesting Generators):** Signature is satisfaction. Strategy is to respond, not initiate. Their enveloping aura attracts opportunities when they

wait for life to come to them. Dating works best when they honor their gut responses rather than chase.

- **Projectors:** Signature is success. Strategy is to wait for the invitation. Projectors' focused aura draws in recognition and invites. Dating calls for patience and discernment— only engage with those who truly see and value you.
- **Reflectors:** Signature is surprise (delight). Strategy is to wait a full lunar cycle before major decisions. Their sampling aura reflects the health of their community. In dating, Reflectors benefit from taking time, observing, and allowing invitations to unfold naturally.

Dating by Design: Love, Invitations, and Saying No

Dating as a Projector was its own biohacking experiment for me. I realized I'd been doing it backwards most of my life — initiating, chasing, trying to prove I was "the one." Sound familiar?

That bitter sting of ghosting or breadcrumbing wasn't bad luck — it was me ignoring my design.

Waiting for Recognition

Projectors are here to be recognized and invited. That means, even in dating, it's not about forcing someone to choose you — it's about noticing who already sees you.

When I started honoring that, everything shifted. Instead of endless swiping, I asked myself:

- Do they see me?
- Do they hear me?
- Do they respect me?
- Do they value me?
- Do I feel genuinely invited to this date or conversation?

- Do I want this, him, her, etc.? (Ego Authority check-in)

If the answer wasn't a full-bodied YES, I let it go — eventually, after learning the painful way, obviously.

The Energy Audit

Dating also became a huge lesson in biohacking: who you let into your aura affects your energy just as much as what you eat or how you sleep. Some dates left me buzzing for hours — others drained me so deeply I needed a full energy reset. This is especially true for those with more open centers than defined ones.

Projectors must steward their energy carefully. This isn't about being picky — it's about being energetically correct.

Lessons Learned

- Decline dates that feel like obligations or "just to be nice."
- Choose meeting spots aligned with your Environment Type (for me, Internal Markets—quiet, curated, selective spaces).
- Stop over-explaining or trying to prove yourself — your aura already says enough.

The result? No more wasted time on mismatched connections. I started attracting higher-quality invitations, and dating became aligned, effortless, and joyful.

(I'm often tempted to write an entire Human Design dating book — but, let's be honest, I don't have the energy for that. Happy to be invited to a podcast, though... hint hint, LOL.)

40

Dating Emotional Generators with Defined Splenic Centers

Let's talk about dating with an open Spleen. Or, more specifically, let's talk about what it's like to date someone with a defined Spleen when you don't have one. Spoiler alert: it can hurt like hell.

Spleen Mechanics 101

In Human Design, the Spleen governs intuition, instinct, immune health, and your sense of safety. When it's defined, a person has a consistent relationship with those signals — their intuitive instinct is steady and reliable, and their presence can literally make other people feel good.

When the Spleen is undefined, like mine, we don't have consistent access to those signals. Instead, we absorb and amplify the Splenic energy of those around us. We become hyper-aware of health, safety, and well-being — but what we feel isn't always ours.

And if you add in an (my) undefined Sacral (life-force/work energy) and undefined Solar Plexus (emotions), you have a recipe for getting completely swept away in someone else's energy and definition.

The Emotional Generator Effect

When I step into the aura of an Emotional Generator with a defined Spleen, it's like standing in an energetic hurricane. Over the past eight years, I've kept a private database of Human Design charts — lovers, friends, clients — and time after time, the ones who brought the most lessons (and heartbreaks) all had the Spleen–Solar Plexus–Sacral trifecta defined.

The Spleen's energy is particularly seductive. You can break up with someone, swear them off — and a week later, you find yourself thinking, *Maybe I overreacted... maybe we should try again.* That false sense of well-being? That's not you — that's your open Spleen still under the influence of their defined one. (You are not weak or crazy, I promise you)

The 3/5 Way Through It

As a 3/5 Profile, I learn by trial and error. So my "field research" has been... extensive:

- A billionaire (financially rich, emotionally bankrupt)
- A man 10 years younger with six-pack abs (hot, but emotionally immature)
- A spiritual guru who was technically homeless (charismatic but chaotic)
- A throuple (spoiler: didn't end well)
- Several failed business collabs that looked good on paper but wrecked my energy
- And, a parent who conditioned me long before I had language for it

What did they all have in common? A defined Spleen.

Every time, I felt incredible around them — safe, grounded, even magnetic. But once I stepped out of their aura (a good 12+ feet away for at least 90 minutes), the magic wore off. It was like coming down from a high and suddenly seeing things clearly.

And to anyone who's ever pulled up next to me at a stoplight and seen me yelling at the sky — no, I wasn't losing it. I was deconditioning.

```
The Biohack for Open Spleen Dating
Here's the hack:
Get distance. Literally. Step away until the
"feel-good" fog clears.
Check in with your own body once you're alone.
If the clarity stays -- it's probably true for you.
If not -- it was just their energy talking.
```

The Takeaway

Open centers aren't flaws — they're where our wisdom lives. But without awareness, they can run our lives. Human Design gave me the tools to discern what's mine and what's just conditioning. And that is the ultimate biohack: reclaiming your energy, your body, and your decisions from the invisible forces that have been running the show.

41

Wealth Without Wellness: The 90-Day Billionaire

Before I share this next story, let's pause on something most biohackers don't talk about enough: the impact of relationships on your biology.

You can have the cleanest supplements, the most dialed-in nutrition, the perfect sleep hygiene — but if your relationships are out of alignment with your values and your design, your body will eventually tell the truth. You can't fake resonance.

As a Projector with seven open centers, my system is finely tuned to pick up energetic signals — both nourishing and depleting. When I found myself dating someone with enormous financial wealth but a complete disconnect from generosity, intimacy, and reciprocity, my body started sounding the alarm.

At first, it was subtle: fatigue, resentment, frustration. But soon I realized this wasn't just about misaligned values — it was a full-body rejection of an energetically incompatible environment. I could almost *feel* my hemoglobin A1c creeping up.

This isn't a money story. It's an energy story. A case study in integrity, self-worth, and the invisible cost of ignoring your Inner Authority.

And yes — there's humor. Because if you can't laugh at your 3/5 trial-and-error, seven open centers, and open-Spleen dating history... are you even living your design?

So here it is: how a billionaire boyfriend helped me biohack my self-worth — and reminded me that sometimes, the most powerful anti-aging hack is walking away.

The 90-Day Billionaire

I once dated a billionaire. I didn't know it at first — though the hints were there: the gated estate, the helipad, the vineyard, the four luxury cars in the garage.

Oddly, dating him didn't feel like dating someone who could buy the planet. It felt like dating a coupon-hoarding minimalist with trust issues.

This man had it all — yet wouldn't spend a single cent unless absolutely necessary. I'm not a gold digger, but after three months of dating, not one nice restaurant. Not even Tony Roma's. Not even Perkins. The man was building a lake in his backyard, but I was eating non-organic Costco leftovers and veggie burgers from Hamburger Habit.

Meanwhile, I'm a Doctor of Psychology with Human Design training, a biological age test in my nightstand, and a nervous system that can feel the difference between organic arugula and a sad bag of Dole mix. And yet here I was, in a house with a private screening room with massage chairs... drinking Kirkland-brand coffee creamer loaded with partially hydrogenated soybean oil. What the...?!

The contrast was jarring.

He would casually talk about "city-building" and "street naming" like it was a hobby. Meanwhile, I was changing the tire on my Smart car and politely asking if we could maybe — just once — go somewhere other than a fluorescent-lit supermarket. The answer was always no. He didn't value experience. He didn't value intimacy. And he definitely didn't value me in a way I could feel.

Here's the thing that shocked me most: billionaires don't get that rich by being generous. They get there by pinching pennies, obsessing over margins, and never tipping. It's not just money — it's an energetic frequency of lack. Scarcity in a gold-plated frame. And I felt it in my body.

My nervous system was fried. My aura felt collapsed. My hormones were staging a rebellion. That's the Human Design biohack right there: when you're not aligned with your values, your biology will rat you out.

The more I saw it clearly — the coffee creamer, the lack of real presence, the matchmaker he'd hired to find me only to ignore what I actually needed — the more obvious it became: it wasn't the frugality. It was the absence of recognition, nourishment, and soul connection.

Projectors (like me) are designed to be invited and recognized. His bank account might have been impressive, but my defined Heart Center was searching for the will to stay.

So I walked away. Not because he was cheap — but because I realized money without health as a priority is just another form of deprivation.

Walking away from the billionaire wasn't the end — it was just the beginning.

Because once I saw the pattern, I realized he wasn't the only one aging me.

The same theme kept showing up in other relationships — and that's where the real deconditioning work began. I need to take full responsibility for me and my part.

Biohacking Your Relationships
Check Your Energy Before & After: How do you feel in someone's presence -- and how do you feel after you leave?
Honor Your Inner Authority: If your gut (or heart, spleen, or ego) says no, trust it -- even if everything "looks good on paper."
Watch Your Biomarkers: Labs don't lie. If your stress hormones, sleep, or weight are tanking, look at who you're spending time with.
Remember: Your biology can't thrive in a relationship that collapses your energy.

42

Phoenix from the Flames

Nothing empowers a person more than the moment you finally rise from heartbreak and feel your internal phoenix take flight.

If I could bottle that moment, I'd be a billionaire.

This is where dark and light meet — where you can only feel the essence of healing light because it's sitting right next to the blackest darkness. And when it happens, it wakes you up — literally and figuratively. You can't force this moment, and you wouldn't volunteer for the pain that comes before it, but when it arrives... it's alchemy.

The Moment Everything Shifts

When the phoenix rises, your life changes in an instant. Suddenly you understand — not just intellectually but viscerally — that transformation can happen at any moment, as soon as you decide.

Yes, the process leading up to that moment might have been slow, grueling, and full of tears. But the actual moment of transformation is instantaneous.

And once it happens, there's no going back.

You are forever altered, because you've tasted freedom. Lying to yourself is no longer an option. You begin to see life differently. Old beliefs and outdated stories fall away like dead skin. The fish that leaps out of the water and sees the shore is never the same fish again.

The Pain Is Temporary

I know it feels like heartbreak will last forever, but that's an illusion. Pain is energy, and energy moves. Some waves move slowly, but they do move.

You may need support — a therapist, a friend, a coach, a "surf instructor" — to help you ride the wave. But you can't bypass it. You can't suppress it. You can't out-think it.

You must feel it.

You have to let the heartbreak have you for a moment so the energy can go somewhere. Avoidance only prolongs the process.

Feel the burn. Let the fire have its way with you.

And when it's done — when it's burned, beaten, and consumed — the seed cracks open.

The Rebirth

This is the moment the phoenix spreads its wings.

Your head rises. You stand taller than ever before. Your perspective shifts to a higher plane. Your breath is deeper. Your nervous system settles into a grounded calm you've never known.

You might even find yourself silent for a while — not because you have nothing to say, but because your energy is speaking louder than words.

And then comes the best part: You feel more like YOU than you ever have before.

Confident. Brave. Calm. Healed.

The old you no longer exists. You're no longer living just to survive heartbreak — you've risen because you chose to rise. You didn't do it to prove anything to anyone. You did it for you.

Once the phoenix landed and I began living from this higher, calmer, more grounded place, I realized something important: **alignment has a cost.** It takes energy, intention, and yes — investment. No one tells you that becoming your truest self often requires rearranging your priorities, your resources, and sometimes your entire life. But here's the truth: the price of alignment is nothing compared to the cost of living out of alignment.

Phoenix Biohacking Tips
Feel It Fully: Don't bypass the pain -- let yourself grieve so the energy can move.
Support Your Body: Sleep, hydrate, nourish yourself, and keep your nervous system steady with breathwork, nature, and movement.
Create Ritual: Mark the moment of your "rebirth" -- journal it, celebrate it, anchor it.
Recognize Your Power: Once you've risen, you know you can never go back to your old ways. Your biology and your spirit both level up.

43

Healer, Heal Thyself - And Other Cool Stuff I Did

Magic Mushrooms: Not My Magic Bullet

Let's start with this: *magic mushrooms suck.* Yeah, I said it. I know there's a mountain of research out there about psilocybin therapy healing trauma and reshaping genetic expressions tied to addiction. But after my own highly scientific (read: chaotic) experimentation, I call BS—*at least for me.*

When I began micro-dosing mushrooms, my goal was to become a glowing statistic validating all that research. Spoiler alert: it didn't work. Why? Because I don't understand the word *"micro."* Micro is a concept that doesn't compute in my macro-loving brain. My attempt at "responsible" mushroom use led me straight back to alcoholism, drug addiction, a torn meniscus, and ultimately crawling back into the 12-step rooms with a fresh Day One chip in hand.

Recovery: The Foundation of Everything Cool

Yes, I'm breaking anonymity here: I'm a recovering alcoholic and addict. For most of my adult life, I've been in and out of recovery—mostly in, with brief forays into the pitiful, incomprehensible demoralization of relapse. Thankfully, the seed of recovery was planted before my 17th birthday. And because I don't have amnesia, I can auto-correct pretty quickly when I veer off course.

The truth is, none of the cool sh*t I've done would've been possible without the foundation of 12-step recovery. My go-to programs? Alcoholics Anonymous (AA), Debtors Anonymous (DA), and Dharma Recovery—a Buddhist-based approach grounded in mindfulness and compassion. Over the years, I've worked several 4th Steps, devoured DA's infamous Yellow Book, and leaned on sponsors who lovingly called me out on my nonsense. These programs gave me community, structure, and—most importantly—peace and serenity.

Breath-work & The Intuitive Healer Era: Crying, Creating, and Healing Together

One of my AA sponsors introduced me to pranayama breath-work. Enter David Elliott, the "reluctant healer," whose two-stage breathing technique cracked open my emotional flood-gates. For the first time in years, I cried—and then promptly became addicted to breath-work, because moderation has never been my strong suit.

I trained with David through all his levels and became a

certified practitioner. Before long, I was leading workshops for sober living homes in Los Angeles, helping people meditate and release emotions they didn't even know they were holding. At one point, David encouraged me to specialize in working with sexual trauma survivors—a path that taught me deep empathy but also led to emotional burnout, thanks in part to my seven open centers in Human Design.

Still, I have no regrets. That season of my life was filled with profound healing—not just for others, but for myself. I feel like I healed alongside my clients during those full moon breath-work circles, especially on that unforgettable New Year's Eve when we filled the yoga studio *twice* in one night. Being able to hold space for people as they breathed, cried, and released what no longer served them was one of the greatest honors of my life. It warms my heart to have been part of so many personal transformations.

Because why stop at breath-work?

During this same time, I launched a creative side hustle that was somewhere between therapy and entrepreneurial chaos. I designed chakra gemstone jewelry, essential oil sprays, eye pillows, and T-shirts—all of which sold out at the chic Fred Segal in LA. My company was called *The Intuitive Healer.* If any of my LA clients are reading this, you might remember those magical full moon meditations we held. It was so rewarding to see people walk into those circles guarded and unsure—and leave transformed, with tear-soaked eye pillows clutched to their chests like sacred relics. That time in my life was wild, raw, beautiful, and deeply fulfilling.

Beyond Step 12: Spiritual Rabbit Holes

After pondering "What comes after Step 12?" (spoiler: Steps 13–24 aren't in the 12-step program), My sister, Cindy gave me a book by, David R. Hawkins' *Transcending the Levels of Consciousness.* This book launched me into a deep dive into vibrational awareness and kinesiology-based muscle testing. Hawkins' work helped me reconcile science with spirituality and craft my own concept of a higher power—a game-changer for this skeptic.

I joined meetups with fellow Hawkins enthusiasts, attended retreats in Santa Barbara, and made lifelong friends who continue to inspire me today. I own and have read cover-to-cover 11 of his books. Again, I don't micro-dose anything—*usually.*

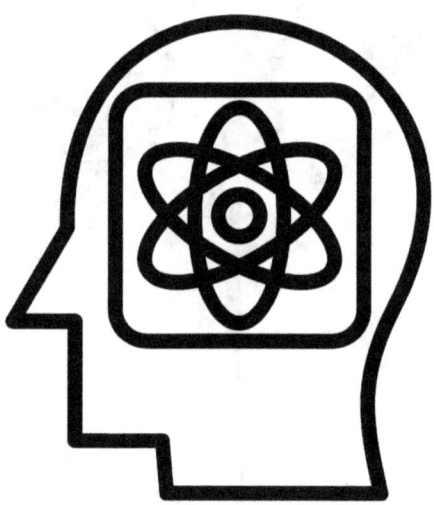

Neuroacoustics: Healing Through Sound

Next up: sound therapy. Dr. Jeffrey Thompson's Neuroacoustic research blew my mind—and naturally, I went all-in. I trained with him, bought his sound therapy chair (yes, it's as cool as it sounds), and incorporated neuroacoustics into my psychotherapy-like coaching practice.

This "talk-then-sound" combo has helped clients heal trauma in as few as nine sessions. During COVID-19 lockdowns, the chair became my personal meditation throne—a biohacking tool *par excellence*. 3D-recorded binaural beats played through a vibrating chair and light glasses take me into theta brainwaves instantly. I call it a meditation hack—so healing, so efficient, and yes, still in my living room if you want to come by for a ride. (Even though it isn't something I advertise on my website.)

Human Design & Destiny Cards

Human Design entered my life like an instruction manual written just for me. With seven open centers in my chart (hello, susceptibility to conditioning), it validated why some work drained me while other pursuits lit me up. And yes — out of all the cool healing sh*t I tried, this one stuck. No need to go deeper here, because... well, you're literally holding the whole book about it.

Then came Rosie Cutter and her **Destiny Cards** — a system for tracking planetary movements and forecasting future possibilities. I'll admit, I was skeptical at first. But over time, I've found them not only entertaining, but also eerily insightful.

For fun, I've been studying the cards and practicing with a few coaching clients at the end of their sessions — if they're open to an amateur reading. The cards are especially useful for forecasting the year ahead, giving a glimpse of what might be unfolding over the next 12 months.

This is a rabbit hole I fully intend to explore more deeply — along with the Gene Keys. Feel free to check in with me if you want to geek out on either of these during a coaching session.

Complex Trauma & Radical Self-Awareness

Here's the kicker: healing complex trauma is... well... complex.

Moving to Florida (thank you, Human Design Strategy!) gave me access to insurance-covered therapy, where I discovered NARM (Neuro Affective Relational Model). The monkey mind of untreated complex trauma is a sneaky beast. Combined with my undefined Head Center and open Emotional Center in Human Design, I'm primed to over-intellectualize as a defense mechanism against actually *feeling* emotions.

My therapist Claude has been incredibly patient—especially since he has full permission to interrupt me any time I start judging myself (which happens constantly, annoying and enlightening).

I also realized how much connection plays a role in healing trauma—not just connection with others but connection with *myself* through contemplative meditation. This practice became my sanctuary—a space where I could observe the monkey mind's gymnastics without getting tangled up in its narrative.

Through therapy and contemplative practices—like talking out loud to myself (thanks to my Ego/Will Center being my inner authority) and meditation—I've learned to pause long enough to actually feel my feelings, rather than run from them or rationalize them away. It's been messy, but worth every second. (And for many people, journaling can be another powerful tool here.)

Final Thoughts: Healing Feels F**king Phenomenal

Yes, I'm a healer—and yes, I've healed myself (mostly). But here's the thing: healing is messy because humans are messy.

Professionals aren't gods; we're just guides doing our best with what we've got.

So take a moment to look in the mirror—or journal about your first memory of shame (fun!). Explore your own journey, because healing—though temporarily painful—is so worth it.

And who knows? You might just discover some cool sh*t along the way, too.

44

Death, Chiron, and I Can't Walk

Conditioning is real. If you're not aware of it, it'll sneak up, take you down, and teach you the hard way. I should know—I've lived it.

I was seduced by other people's auras. I ignored my strategy and authority. And then my Chiron Return showed up like a cosmic wrecking ball. This was during the celery juice era, when people thought blending greens and joining "That Girl Group" would solve everything. And yes, it was fun—about 51% of the time. The other 49%? A swirling cocktail of edibles, Adderall, alcohol, mushrooms, and ketamine, all disguised as spiritual exploration and ecstatic dance.

Let me be clear: I take full responsibility for my choices—and for being a conditioning force in other people's lives, especially when under the influence. But accountability often comes *after* the damage is done. I can't count how many times I've heard:

"Julie, you're too much."

"Julie, you can't see my wife anymore—you're a bad influence."

Am I ashamed or proud? Honestly, I still don't know. (Insert evil laugh.)

A Recipe for Chaos: My Human Design + Substances

(Do as I say, not as I do.)

As a Projector with seven open centers and my only defined channel being 25–51 (the Channel of Shock), I came here to deliver big medicine… and sometimes big chaos. My Incarnation Cross is the Right Angle Cross of Penetration. That's not subtle. My aura penetrates. I shock. Add mind-altering substances into that mix and you've got a full-blown energetic tornado.

I've been uninvited to weddings. Rockstars and film producers have texted me to tell me to leave their lives (and their partners) alone. Being a 3/5 Profile — the "Martyr-Heretic" — means I learn by trial and error and often live out loud: either projected onto as a savior or burned at the stake. There's very little middle ground.

Here's the blunt lesson: if you have a 5 in your profile, casual use of alcohol or other substances rarely stays casual. This isn't moralizing — it's design and hard experience talking. Substances that fog your awareness are not friends if you want to age well, stay resilient, and biohack with intention.

Remember the whole "red wine is good for your heart" narrative? It's crumbling. The biohacking community now admits what many of us felt: alcohol is not a longevity tool. If you're drinking for resveratrol, take the supplement and stop kidding yourself. (Said with love, and a truckload of lived experience.)

My chaos looked like late nights, too-many parties, colorful friend groups, dancing, and an openness to experimenting with substances. The crescendo of that season wasn't glamorous — it culminated in a relapse and, not long after, a torn meniscus. One morning I literally couldn't walk. That sudden immobility felt like a divine stop sign: the universe putting a full-body *NO MORE* in bright neon.

That injury forced me to pause in a way nothing else could. It was humiliation and mercy wrapped together. I did the experimenting so you don't have to: yes, I tested the edges, and yes, I fell hard. Learn from it. If you want to biohack for longevity, clarity, and real alignment, substances that erode awareness are mostly liabilities, not tools.

So yeah — I bring the medicine, and sometimes I bring the chaos. I share both because both taught me how to come back to myself. If you're following my roadmap, take the detour: skip the drama, keep your nervous system intact, and prioritize the long game. Your future self will thank you.

April 23rd: My Chiron Return + Miles' Birthday

My nephew Miles was originally due on my birthday, April 7th. But he was stillborn on April 23rd—my exact Chiron Return date, 2019. The timing broke something in me. It also made me question everything.

My sister is writing a book about grief, and I know I'll be a cautionary tale in it—the doctor of psychology who *didn't* do it right. I won't share more out of respect for her, her husband, and Miles' memory. I only mention it here because the synchronicity of it all, I'm still processing.

Enter the Medium: "You Are Not Supported"

Around that time, I visited my friend Riz, a Medium who channels Red Eagle. I limped into the session, still unable to walk properly. Red Eagle looked at me and said, "This is a symbol. You are not supported. Not by the people currently in your life. And this pattern began when you were 14."

He was right. The "girls" didn't have my back. And neither did I. I'd left behind the support of the 12-step rooms, my therapist, and my sober network. Instead, I turned to a group of spiritual by passers with drugs in their pockets and plant medicine plans in the jungle—with no aftercare.

Later I was on the other side of the office when one of my life coaching clients spent 18 months unraveling what came up in *his* unsupervised plant medicine journey. That kind of work requires integration and support. Without it, you risk trauma, not healing.

The Meniscus Wake-Up Call

Tearing my meniscus turned out to be a blessing—because it forced me to stop and listen. I dove deep into the world of inflammation, eliminated sugar (RIP ketchup), started drinking red clover tea, and found ways to sneak apple cider vinegar into my body without gagging. But the biggest shift happened when I got a second opinion from a surgeon.

He said, "I've got the same tear. You can either start swimming and spinning, or I can cut out healthy tissue and you'll likely get arthritis."

Nope. No surgery for me. Swimming became my "thing"—and by swimming, I mean flailing around for 30 minutes. But I bike nearly every day now, and I protect my knee like it's made of gold. No high heels. No long hikes. No heavy purses.

This injury slowed me down, but it also made me smarter. More deliberate. More tuned in and severely increased my body awareness.

Final Thoughts: Awareness is the Ultimate Anti-Aging Tool

Every hard moment—Miles' death, Chiron Return, the injury, the psychedelic detour—taught me something. Every breakdown opened a door to new biohacking wisdom and deeper self-awareness.

This journey is messy, yes. But it's mine. And if I can leave you with one thing, it's this:

Healing isn't just about protocols and supplements. It's about awareness, support, and learning how to say "no" to what isn't aligned.

When you know better, you do better.

And sometimes, you also bike more and give up heels.

45

You Have to Be a Warrior

You have to fight for your vitality.

You have to fight for your clarity.

You have to fight for your life.

No one else can do it for you.

This entire book has been about reclaiming your biology, your energy, and your agency. And that is the essence of being a warrior — specifically, a **spiritual warrior**.

What It Really Means to Be a Spiritual Warrior

People often ask me what that term means. I even answered this question during a podcast interview with Lia Montelongo, the co-founder of *Spiritual Warrior World* (and one of the original Mortal Kombat characters, by the way — talk about a real-life warrior!).

Here's my distilled answer:

A spiritual warrior is someone who faces the mental, emotional, and physical challenges of life with courage, self-awareness, and a commitment to growth. It's not about never falling — it's about getting back up. It's about integrating the mess, choosing to keep moving, and (as I like to say) wiping the sh*t off and marching forward with class.

We've all faced hardship, heartbreak, trauma, and fear. Many of us have coped with addictive behaviors along the way — I certainly have. But being a spiritual warrior isn't about perfection. It's about resilience. It's about finding your way back to yourself, again and again, even when you've gotten lost.

The Internal Work: Showing Up for Yourself

We are taught to show up for others — to be loyal, responsible, and accountable. But how often do we turn that loyalty inward?

Being a spiritual warrior means building that trust with yourself. It means staying true to your values even when the world tempts you to abandon them. That's not easy. In fact, it's some of the hardest work you'll ever do.

The Rites of Passage

When you truly commit to living in alignment, life will ask you to take bold action:

- Ending relationships that no longer serve you
- Leaving jobs that stifle your spirit
- Saying no to what's easy so you can say yes to what's true
- Cutting out addictions (sugar, alcohol, social media, perfectionism) that keep you numb

These are not just choices — they are initiations. They are the trials that forge your inner strength.

Human Design: The Warrior's Toolkit

For me, Human Design is one of the most powerful tools for spiritual resilience. It gives you a map back to yourself:

- **Strategy & Authority** → The compass that points you toward decisions that strengthen, not weaken, you.
- **Environment & Digestion** → The day-to-day mechanics that allow your biology to regenerate and your cells to feel safe.
- **Open Centers & Deconditioning** → The practice of releasing conditioning so you can stop living by someone else's script.

When you live in alignment with your design, you become stronger — physically, mentally, emotionally. Your digestion improves. Your sleep deepens. Your relationships shift. And yes, you even age more slowly.

Choosing Your Truth

In today's hyper-connected world, it is easier than ever to abandon yourself — to let algorithms, cultural expectations, and other people's opinions dictate who you should be. Being a spiritual warrior means resisting that pull. It means saying:

"This is who I am. This is how I live. This is my truth."

That choice is radical. That choice builds real self-esteem — the kind no supplement, no social media like, and no external validation can give you.

Joining the Movement

When I was invited to join Spiritual Warrior World, I hesitated. I knew I would bring intensity, ask big questions, and challenge the status quo. But the team said yes — they wanted that energy. And I realized: this is what we need more of. Spaces where we can be fully awake, fully alive, fully aligned.

So here's my invitation to you: **join me.** Not just literally — though you're welcome to — but in spirit. Be the kind of person who chooses alignment over approval. Who listens to your body over the noise of the world. Who rises from the ashes, again and again, with clarity, courage, and humor intact.

Because the truth is, you don't just have to be a biohacker to live a long, vital life.

You have to be a warrior.

Corporate & Collective Applications

And this isn't just personal. Incorporating Human Design into corporate workshops has changed the game for many of my clients. When teams learn their Type, Strategy, Authority—and even aura dynamics—meetings run smoother, burnout drops, and collaboration skyrockets. People start respecting how different colleagues operate, rather than expecting everyone to work the same way.

Imagine what could happen if every workplace gave their employees permission to follow their Strategy and Authority. Productivity would go up, but so would well-being.

My Personal Biohacking Wins

Here's how I've applied Human Design to my own life:

- I stopped trying to keep up with Generators and let myself rest as a Projector—avoiding the burnout that used to be my norm.
- I spent more time in my correct environment (Internal Markets), and my energy came roaring back.
- I honored my Indirect Light digestion and started eating after sunset—my sleep, labs, and body composition all improved.
- I layered those insights with targeted supplementation, hormone balancing, and fasting protocols designed for women in menopause.

The result? My biological age dropped by two full years—confirmed by a cheek-swab test from a Harvard-affiliated lab.

But here's the truth: this book isn't about my experiment.

It's an invitation for yours.

Your Invitation to Experiment

You don't have to do everything at once—just start. Learn your Type, your Strategy, your Authority. Pick one experiment. Run it for two weeks. See how you feel. Then try another.

You don't have to get it perfect; you just have to get curious. Your body will tell you when something is working. Your life will tell you when you're in alignment.

And who knows? You might just get younger in the process.

Final Word — And Invitation

You've just read my playbook—equal parts Human Design, biohacking, and battle scars. Now it's your turn.

Run your chart. Learn your Type, Strategy, and Authority. Start one experiment. Notice what shifts.

And if you want a guide along the way, I'd love to support you. You can book a Human Design immersion, a biohacking coaching session, or even bring me in for a corporate workshop. The next step is yours.

You are the experiment.

You are the biohack.

You are the warrior.

Thank you.

46

Your Turn to Hack Aging — Your Way

If you've made it to the end of this book, first—**congratulations**. You've just traveled through a blend of Human Design, biohacking, psychology, and a few cheeky stories that prove real transformation is never just theoretical. It's lived. It's messy. And it's uniquely yours.

My hope is that somewhere between cheek swabs and Human Design charts, between naps and strategy, between digestion experiments and dating stories, you started to recognize the quiet power of **living according to your design**.

Because when you stop fighting your nature and start aligning with it, something extraordinary happens:

Your biology listens.

Your energy expands.

Your aging process slows down.

And your life starts to feel like it actually fits.

Human Design gave me the lens. Biohacking gave me the tools. Psychology gave me the language. And humor made the whole thing not just bearable, but joyful. That's the alchemy I want for you, too.

You don't need to mimic someone else's routine or live by "expert" hacks that don't fit. Your chart already holds the map. Your body holds the truth. And the experiment is yours to run.

And for my beloved Generators—the steady engines of this world—you are often the ones waiting for guidance to respond to. You make up the majority of the population and, truthfully, the majority of my clients. Working with Generators has been one of the most rewarding parts of my journey. When Projectors and Generators find the right rhythm together, the results are powerful.

An Invitation

If you're ready to take this work deeper—whether personally or professionally—I'd love to support you.

Work with me 1:1 — Book a private Human Design Biohacking session or psychological life coaching container and let's design a longevity road map that's truly yours.

Book me to speak — Bring Human Design-informed bio-hacking and psychological insight to your company, conference, or community. I offer keynotes and experiential workshops that educate, inspire, and invite people to see themselves—and each other—through a more accurate and compassionate lens.

Stay connected — Visit DrJulieK.com for resources, events, and ways to collaborate.

The truth is, you're not here to hack aging like anyone else. You're here to **hack aging like you**—with your unique design, your unique body, and your unique story.

So go ahead. Run your experiments. Be curious. Rest when you need to. Laugh often. And remember: getting younger isn't about chasing time—it's about finally living in alignment with yourself. Here's to your next chapter—vibrant, aligned, and beautifully, unmistakably you.

VIII

References & Resources

47

References

ScienceDirect. (n.d.). Social connectedness. In ScienceDirect Topics. Retrieved September 22, 2025, from https://www.scie ncedirect.com/topics/psychology/social-connectedness

BG5 Business Institute. (n.d.). Free chart reports. https://bg5 businessinstitute.com/chart-reports/free

Bulletproof. (n.d.). Bulletproof coffee recipe. https://www.bul letproof.com/recipes/bulletproof-diet-recipes/bulletproof-c offee-recipe/

International Human Design School. (n.d.). International Human Design School (IHD School). https://ihdschool.com/

Jovian Archive. (n.d.). Human Design and Ra Uru Hu. https://w ww.jovianarchive.com/human_design/rauruhu

Maia Mechanics Imaging. (n.d.). Maia Mechanics chart

software. https://www.maiamechanics.com/

Montelongo, L. (Host). (n.d.). Spiritual Warrior World Podcast. Facebook. https://www.facebook.com/groups/EgoProjectorsInitiation

NARM Training Institute. (n.d.). What is NARM?. https://narmtraining.com/what-is-narm/

Nourishing Wellness. (n.d.). Nourishing wellness. https://nourishingwellness.com/

PLOS Medicine. (2010). Study on health behaviors and mortality. PLOS Medicine, 7(7), e1000316. https://doi.org/10.1371/journal.pmed.1000316

Ra TV. (n.d.). Ra Uru Hu lectures and media. https://www.ra.tv/

Saladino, P. (n.d.). PaulSaladino,MD. https://www.paulsaladinomd.co/

Sinclair, D. (n.d.). TallyHealth. https://tallyhealth.com/

The DNA Company. (n.d.). Genetic testing and personalized health insights. https://thednacompany.com/

Pelz, M.(n.d.). Fastlikeagirl. https://fastlikeagirl.com/

ScienceDirect. (2022). Study on longevity and metabolic health. Cell ReportsMedicine,3(7). https://doi.org/10.1016/j.xcrm.2022.100031

Somers,S.(2009). Ageless:Thenakedtruthaboutbioidenticalho
rmones. NewYork,NY:CrownArchetype.

WellnessandGrief.(2019,November4).5hardtruthsaboutstillbi
rthloss.Retrievedfromhttps://www.wellnessandgrief.com/po
st/2019/11/04/5-hard-truths-about-stillbirth-loss

48

Resources

JovianArchive–Official site for HumanDesign teachings and materials fromRaUruHu.

InternationalHumanDesignSchool–Global training hub for certifiedHumanDesigneducation.

MaiaMechanics – Advanced chart software and tools forHumanDesignanalysis.

BG5BusinessInstitute–Professional and career applications of HumanDesign.

RaTV–Streaming library ofRaUruHulectures and educa-tionalmedia.

EgoProjectorsInitiationGroup – Community platform forEgoProjectors.

ScienceDirect–Academic database for psychology and humanbehavior topics.

TallyHealth–Biologicalagetestingandlongevityrecommendati
ons.

TheDNACompany–Genetictestingandpersonalizedhealthrepo
rts.

FastLikeaGirl–Dr.MindyPelz'sfastingmethodologyforwomen
.

NourishingWellness–Functionalnutritionandlifestylemedici
neresources.

PaulSaladino,MD–Animal-basednutritionandmetabolichealt
heducation.

BulletproofCoffeeRecipe–OriginalMCT-oilandbuttercoffeefor
mulation.

PLOSMedicineStudy–Researchonhealthbehaviorsandmortali
tyoutcomes.

ScienceDirectStudy–Researchonlongevityandmetabolicfunct
ion.

NARMTraining–Trauma-healingandNeuroAffectiveRelationa
lModelresources.

AlcoholicsAnonymous–Peersupportforsobrietyandaddictionr
ecovery.

Wellness&Grief–Articlesandresourcesforgriefandemotionalh
ealing.

EnvironmentalWorkingGroup(EWG)–Productsafetyandingre
dienttransparency.

RecoveryDharma–Mindfulness-basedprogramforaddictionre
covery.

DebtorsAnonymous–Supportgroupforfinancialandbehaviora
lrecovery.

VeritasPublishing–Spiritualandeducationalbooksandmedia.

Dr.JulieK–NeuroAcousticMusicStoreandwellnesssessions.

RizMirza–Channelingandspiritualdevelopmentteachings.

SpiritualWarriorWorld–Onlinecommunityandpodcastforspiri
tualgrowth.

About the Author

Dr. Julie Kokesch, Psy.D.

Doctor of Psychology, Human Design Advisor, Author, Speaker

Dr. Julie Kokesch, known as **Dr. Julie K.**, is a seasoned Doctor of Psychology with over 20 years of experience in the personal development field. She holds a Bachelor's degree in Psychology from UCLA and both a Master's and Doctorate in Clinical Psychology from Ryokan College. Her doctoral dissertation, *"The Psychological Manifestations of Internet Addiction in the Digital Native Population,"* has been widely recognized and presented at graduate-level lectures.

Throughout her career, Dr. Julie has contributed her expertise at a range of respected institutions, including the Gay & Lesbian Center in Hollywood, CA, a private drug and alcohol rehabilitation facility in Malibu, and an outpatient treatment center for teens and families. She has also made media appearances on TLC's *My Strange Addiction*, *The Dr. Phil House*, and numerous podcasts, sharing her insights with wider audiences.

Over the past decade, Dr. Julie has integrated her deep psychological background with **Human Design**, completing advanced training through the International Human Design School. She brings this knowledge to her work as a Human Design educator and facilitator, and in 2025 presented at the High Desert Human Design Conference in Santa Fe, NM. Dr. Julie's signature approach blends psychology, Human Design, and humor—drawing on her experience as a retired professional stand-up comedian—to create engaging, transformative workshops. She currently leads in-person Human Design sessions in Miami Beach, facilitates compatibility workshops, and offers corporate training for teams. She is also a founding member of *A Human Design Experience*, which will host its inaugural South Florida conference in April 2026.

In addition to her work in psychology and Human Design, Dr. Julie is trained in **NeuroAcoustics with a specialization in Psycho-Sensory Integration**, offering therapeutic music through her online store. Her background also includes leading Pranayama breath work groups and running a boutique wellness store.

Blending the scientific with the experiential, Dr. Julie integrates **psychology, biohacking, and Human Design** to offer a unique and personalized path to transformation. She continues to provide virtual coaching to clients worldwide.

You can connect with me on:

🌐 https://www.drjuliek.com

🐦 https://www.linkedin.com/in/coachdrjuliek

📘 https://www.facebook.com/DrJulieK

Subscribe to my newsletter:

✉ https://lp.constantcontactpages.com/su/q0PPPV1/book

* 9 7 9 8 2 1 8 8 3 5 2 8 6 *